Interpreting the Play Script

Contemplation and Analysis

Anne Fliotsos

D0024219

palgrave
macmillan

First published 2011 by
PALGRAVE MACMILLAN

Palgrave Macmillan in the UK is an imprint of Macmillan Publishers Limited,
registered in England, company number 785998, of Houndmills, Basingstoke,
Hampshire RG21 6XS.

Palgrave Macmillan in the US is a division of St Martin's Press LLC,
175 Fifth Avenue, New York, NY 10010.

Palgrave Macmillan is the global academic imprint of the above companies
and has companies and representatives throughout the world.

Palgrave® and Macmillan® are registered trademarks in the United States,
the United Kingdom, Europe and other countries.

ISBN: 978–0–230–29003–7 hardback
ISBN: 978–0–230–29004–4 paperback

This book is printed on paper suitable for recycling and made from fully
managed and sustained forest sources. Logging, pulping and manufacturing
processes are expected to conform to the environmental regulations of the
country of origin.

A catalogue record for this book is available from the British Library.

A catalog record for this book is available from the Library of Congress.

10 9 8 7 6 5 4 3 2 1
20 19 18 17 16 15 14 13 12 11

Printed in China

"I am convinced that this book will become an important text for studies in play and script analysis. It promises to draw in various levels of students and theatre practitioners because of its unique introduction of inner contemplation via Zen philosophy and practice. It also lays possibly new and interesting groundwork for further exploration into successful script analysis and acting."

Gail Medford, *Professor of Theatre Arts, Bowie State University, Maryland*

"*Interpreting the Play Script* has a great deal to offer teachers and students interested in analyzing contemporary plays that do not use traditional forms. It is the first book I have seen that devotes significant space to identifying serious methods of analyzing unconventional plays, alongside the most useful methods of traditional script analysis. I have long been looking for just such a text to use in my courses – one that helps to rigorously develop the artist's response to a script."

Shelley Orr, Lecturer, San Diego State University and Past President, Literary Managers and Dramaturgs of the Americas

The starting point for virtually all theatre is studying the play script, but what does this involve? *Interpreting the Play Script: Contemplation and Analysis* argues that one type of analysis cannot fit every play, nor does one method suit every theatre artist or collaborative team. The first text to combine traditional and non-traditional models, it gives students a range of tools with which to approach different kinds of performance.

Supported by pragmatic questions, practical exercises and sources for further reading, this book will challenge students and theatre practitioners to engage with the play using both analysis and contemplation. It is essential reading for anyone wanting to unlock and more fully understand the performance potential of any play.

Anne Fliotsos is Associate Professor of Theatre at Purdue University, Indiana, USA. Her publications include *Teaching Theatre Today: Pedagogical Views of Theatre in Higher Education* (2nd edition) and *American Women Stage Directors of the 20th Century*.

Also by Anne Fliotsos

Teaching Theatre Today: Pedagogical Views of Theatre in Higher
   Education (*with Gail S. Medford*)
American Women Stage Directors of the Twentieth Century (*with
   Wendy Vierow*)

*To the professors, students, and colleagues who have challenged
me to think in new ways and walk new paths*

Contents

List of Figures

Acknowledgments

The author and publishers wish to thank the following for permission to reproduce copyright material:

Anita Evans for DirectorsLabChicago photo by Anita Evans (2010)

Bud Coleman for Zen Rock Garden photo by Bud Coleman (2010)

Elsevier for excerpts from "Action Analysis," pp. 1–36, from James Thomas, *Script Analysis for Actors, Directors, and Designers*. 4th ed., Focal Press/Elvesier (2009)

Harold Ober Associates, Inc. for pp. 23–24, from Michael Mayer's translation of Henrik Ibsen, *A Doll's House* in *Ghosts and Three Other Plays*, Anchor Books (1966, 1994)

Nick Hern for excerpts from Kenneth McLeish's translation of Aristotle, *Poetics*, TCG (1999), originally published by Nick Hern Books

Purdue Theatre for *The Seagull* photo by Stephanie Paine. Directed by Gordon McCall (2008)

Salvage Vanguard Theater for *Venus* photo by Sarah Bork Hamilton. Play by Suzan-Lori Parks, directed by Jason Neulander at Salvage Vanguard Theater (1999)

Theatre Communications Group for excerpts from Anne Bogart and Tina Landau, *The Viewpoints Book: A Practical Guide to Viewpoints and Composition*, TCG (2005)

University of Michigan Press, for excerpts from Gerald F. Else's translation of Aristotle's *Aristotle: Poetics*, University of Michigan Press (1967)

William Morris Endeavor Entertainment, LLC, for Suzan-Lori Parks, *Venus*, Dramatists Play Service (1995, 1998). Copyright © 1995 by Suzan-Lori Parks.

Every effort has been made to trace rights holders, but if any have been inadvertently overlooked, the publishers would be pleased to make the necessary arrangements at the first opportunity.

Preface

Interpreting the Play Script: Contemplation and Analysis begins with an argument that one type of analysis cannot fit every play, nor does one interpretive model suit every artist or collaborative team. There are several script analysis books in the market, though most are distressingly similar, advocating a single approach and vocabulary – usually a derivative of Aristotle's, Freytag's, Stanislavski's principles. Many authors start with the most basic elements: What is theatre? What is a script? I leave that kind of discussion to introductory theatre textbooks. Here, my audience consists of theatre students and practitioners who are familiar with basic concepts and are ready to create theatre, which requires them to articulate their personal interpretations in a collaborative, evolving process. This book fills a gap by providing a variety of lenses through which to examine and interpret a script, considering both subjective and objective responses to the text.

In my own teaching of a graduate course in script interpretation, attention to intuitive contemplation of the script alongside more traditional analytical methods has been successful with student-artists.[1] This approach agrees well with Howard Gardner's theory of Multiple Intelligences (MI), for it acknowledges that each of us has a distinct intellectual profile, and that teachers must teach to different intelligences in order to enhance student learning.[2] Although a purely analytical approach is appropriate for those who have a strong logical intelligence, contemplative and intuitive approaches resonate with those who have higher intrapersonal intelligence. The specific exercises in this book also appeal to bodily-kinesthetic and spatial intelligence, which are so often heightened in actors, directors, and designers.

Opening up our modes of interpretation also makes sense in light of the changes in dramaturgy over the centuries. Although

Aristotle's, Freytag's, and Stanislavski's analytical techniques work well with realism and linear plays, playwrights have been reacting to realism and crafting alternative forms of performance for more than a century. At the turn of the twenty-first century, idiosyncratic playwrights such as Suzan-Lori Parks and Charles Mee explored postmodern methods of script construction, often without realistic settings of time or place, let alone causal progression of action, psychologically driven characters, or literal dialogue. Trying to interpret such nonlinear plays through an Aristotelian lens is rather like trying to pound a square peg into a round hole.

The sections of this book are presented in an order that best suits my students: starting from a point of intuitive and initial subjective response (Part I), moving to familiar traditional/intellectual methods of analysis (Part II), then reflecting on alternative methods for nonlinear scripts (Part III). Because Part III also reflects back to Part I, you may also choose to start with traditional analysis, then move on to Parts I and III, or simply use the sections individually. Just as there is no one "right" way to approach a script, this text may be used in any manner that best suits a class or an individual artist.

Because this book deals in personal experiences and reflection, I have adopted a first and second person form of address. I have avoided weighing the reader down with lengthy explanations, esoteric theory, or copious examples, opting instead for a straightforward, concise approach. Given that the book introduces a number of techniques and philosophies, it is important that readers ground their individual understanding through additional reading and practice. For ease of reference, a summary of major questions and sources for further study are provided at the end of each section.

This book has benefited greatly from the help of theatre professors who have responded to my conference presentations and early drafts. I would especially like to thank Anne Fletcher, Cheryl Black, Jeannie Woods, Gail Medford, Wendy Vierow, Bob W. Johnson, Kristine Holtvedt, and Richard Stockton Rand for their comments and encouragement. My gratitude also goes to those who helped provide photographs, including Bud Coleman, Jenny

Larson, Sarah Bork Hamilton, Anita Evans, David Lageveen, and Liz Krane. I am indebted to editor Kate Haines and her staff as well as the readers of the manuscript, all of whom provided valuable advice and support throughout the process of revision and production. Finally, many thanks to my students for their feedback on the early version of the book and on applying the techniques therein. I am heartened by their support and delighted by their personal discoveries.

Notes

1. For further information, see also my essay "From Script Analysis to Script Interpretation: Valorizing the Intuitive." *Theatre Topics* 19.2 (September 2009): 153–63.
2. See Gardner's original groundbreaking work, *Frames of Mind: The Theory of Multiple Intelligences* (New York: Basic Books, 1983) or his updated book, *Multiple Intelligences: New Horizons* (New York: Basic Books, 2006). Gardner's intelligences include musical, bodily-kinesthetic, logical-mathematical, linguistic, spatial, interpersonal, intrapersonal, and naturalist.

Introduction

The starting point for the vast majority of theatre productions is the study of the script, but what should such study include? Identifying the protagonist and antagonist? Finding the exposition, rising action, climax, and resolution? Deriving the central idea or spine of the play? Recording your own visceral impressions of the play? Researching the playwright and time period? Is there, in fact, one ideal approach, or are there a variety of utilitarian and artistic approaches?

This book provides several lenses through which an artist can examine a script. Although formalist analysis has traditionally been the Western approach to scripts – compliments of Aristotle, Stanislavski, and a few others – it cannot and should not be the only lens. After several years of teaching a course in graduate script analysis, I asked myself: How can I open up the realm of examining scripts by incorporating alternative perspectives to counter and/or complement intellectual analysis? How might a focus on intuitive response and deep contemplation of the script transform students who are taught to categorize and analyze? English professor Mary Rose O'Reilley reflects on the dichotomy of the two approaches in her book *The Peaceable Classroom*, writing, "When I am in my critiquing mind, I am not as tranquil as when I am in my pondering mind. My claws are at the veins of life. When I am comparing, I am not contemplating essential beauty" (92). Theatre practitioners interpreting a script need to understand and develop both "minds" in order to give themselves fully to the act of interpretation.

With these concepts in mind, *Interpreting the Play Script* reveals that one type of analysis cannot do justice to a play, nor does one interpretive lens suit every theatre artist or collaborative team.

The book comprises four parts, which may be read separately or out of order:

I. Contemplation and intuitive response, including Zen philosophy.
II. Formalist analysis, via Aristotle, Freytag, and Stanislavski.
III. Interpreting the non-linear play: frames of reference.
IV. Responding to the script: choosing a path of interpretation.

Each part includes practical exercises and questions for study and application, geared to students and artists in production. Examples are primarily from three different scripts: Sophocles' *Oedipus Rex,* Ibsen's *A Doll's House,* and Mel Brooks's Broadway musical, *The Producers.* The brief concluding section helps the student/practitioner formulate a response to the script, while keeping an open mind about discoveries to be made in the production process. Ultimately, the reader will be able to answer two crucial questions: How do I bring both objective and subjective responses to my interpretation of the script? How can I create a personal response which best communicates my reaction to and understanding of this script?

By advocating not one approach, but contemplating various approaches to the script, I hope this book will foster in readers a deeper understanding of their relationship with their art – be it as directors, actors, designers or the myriad of others who work to produce theatre.

Reference

O'Reilley, Mary Rose. *The Peaceable Classroom.* Portsmouth, NH: Heinemann, 1993.

I

Contemplation and Intuitive Response

Responding to art: an introduction

When we sit down and listen to a piece of music, what is our immediate reaction? Most likely, we have an emotional response of some kind. For example, listening to the overture to a classic musical comedy, such as *The Music Man,* would likely give us a sense of lightness and frivolity. We may also have a physical response, such as tapping a beat. We may see images or sense colors, and the music may transport us to a specific setting through our mind's eye. These responses are natural and intuitive. We allow ourselves to react wholly, as human beings.

If we have studied music, a set of different reactions may also arise, which link to our intellectual responses. If we feel a sense of lightness and frivolity, we realize that the key in which the music is written is a factor, as is the tempo, the melody, and a number of other variables. Our physical desire to tap our toes likely stems from the rhythm of the music, or perhaps a driving down beat. Images from the lyrics may stem from metaphors or other poetic devices. For each of these reactions, we can look to both the subjective and objective information that we gather when we interpret music through ourselves. We bring both technical information about music – structure, chords, rhythms, etc. – and intuitive information from our visceral reactions to the music. One approach is not right and one wrong, nor is one necessarily more "worthy" than the other, but by considering both aspects we get a fuller, deeper understanding of the music and how it engages our mind-body-spirit. This need for both the logical and intuitive approach to art is fundamental to understanding and discussing any art form.

As students and artists of the theatre, it makes sense for us to hone not only our technical and analytical skills, but also to contemplate our intuitive impressions. Because we each see a play from our own unique perspective, based upon our personal outlook, experiences, training, and cognitive predispositions, we will have different experiences encountering art. The astonishing variety of individual interpretation makes working in the arts invigorating, but it can also be frustrating as we try to collaborate. As theatre artists and collaborators, we need to cultivate and balance our skills as we approach a script or a play in development. A theatre artist who analyzes the script but ignores his or her intuitive response is doomed to mediocrity. In "Reading the Dramatic Text For Production," professor Julian M. Olf saw this phenomenon among his students: "The same students who could offer articulate, critical exegeses on the most subtle aspects of the dramatic text were often those who suffered from an antiseptic, nonvisceral orientation to the work; their approaches to production – whether as actors, directors, dramaturgs, or designers – were often lackluster if not outright boring" (153). In a similar vein, dramaturg Geoffrey S. Proehl argues that artists need not only knowledge, but also an understanding of the script. In *Toward a Dramaturgical Sensibility: Landscape and Journey* (2008), he explains, "Understanding allows for a way of knowing that is deeper, slower, more holistic. It indicates an approach to analysis that uses as much of the self as possible, not only the left side of the brain" (89).

Combining such different approaches, very broadly construed as the subjective and the objective, brings to mind the concept of *yin* and *yang*. In Chinese philosophy, yin–yang incorporates two opposite forces (thesis/antithesis), forming a whole and ever-changing relationship between the two dichotomies

Figure I.1 Yin–yang symbol

(see Figure I.1). Neither force has complete dominance, but exists in a position relative to the other, constantly relating in a cyclical pattern.[1]

Intuitive response and theatre: seeing with an "inner eye"

The subjective experience has long been a part of creating theatre, particularly in reactions against realism and naturalism. At the turn of the twentieth century, playwrights and theorists of nonrealistic movements argued that exploring the inner, hidden life within us all is more important than the exterior, day-to-day events of reality. For example, playwright Maurice Maeterlinck's symbolist plays from the turn of the twentieth century center on "inner action," which lies under the surface of everyday reality. Metaphor, intuition, and spirituality have more bearing in Maeterlinck's plays than cause-and-effect action. In a similar vein, Antonin Artaud grew tired of the storytelling tradition of theatre, based on text, and proposed a Theatre of Cruelty, one that assaulted the audiences' senses and reached an inner core, beyond the intellect. By the late twentieth century, postmodern-ist Robert Wilson sought to warp the audiences' conception of time and space on stage in order to reach the audiences' "inner screen," a semi-consciousness state.[2]

Though known for his concrete actor-training techniques and approaches to the script, Konstantin Stanislavski spent much of his career delving into the mystical link among body, mind, and spirit, though Soviet censors kept this aspect of his work hidden. By the end of his career, Stanislavski was convinced that intel-lectual exploration of the text was not enough. Yoga became a required exercise for Stanislavski's actors – a gateway to connect-ing the mind-body-spirit – a path from which to enter a "crea-tive state" (Wegner 85). Influenced by Hinduism, Stanislavski and other Soviet director-theorists such as Eugene Vakhtangov and Michael Chekhov sought to find the inner energy of the actor and bring it to the audience. Actor Vera Solovovia recalled, "We worked a great deal on concentration. It was called 'To get into the circle.' We imagined a circle around us and sent 'prana' rays of communion into space and to each other"[3] (quoted in Wegner 86). Through new research and translation of his work, Stanislavski's reliance on mystical, holistic approaches to acting are finally coming to light.[4]

Reflective learning and contemplative practice

The idea that introspection or personal reflection plays an impor-tant role in learning is not new. For example, educational theorist John Dewey was writing about it in the early twentieth century in *How We Think: A Restatement of the Relation of Reflective Thinking to the Educative Process*, arguing that linear models of thinking were restrictive. Dewey applies his progressive thinking in his book *Art As Experience* as well, arguing, "the roots of aesthetic experience ... lie in commonplace experience, in the consumma-tory experiences that are ubiquitous in the course of human life" (Field n.p.). In essence, Dewey refers to archetypal patterns and behaviors, those connecting us all in a web of human experi-ences; one might say this is the essence of humanity that binds us all. If art is a refection of the human condition, it makes sense that introspection and personal reflection should be the foundation of reacting to a work of art as well as the foundation of creating one.[5]

In terms of reacting to art, the consideration of both intuitive response and critical analysis helps accommodate our individual differences in processing information. Learning theory has long held that students learn best through different modes: for example, some learners respond more to aural stimuli and others to visual stimuli. Roger Sperry's studies in the 1960s focused on a right-brain (abstract thinking) and left-brain (logical thinking) dichotomy, though since that time psychologists have moved beyond this simple dichotomy to explore more complex theories. There are numerous studies about brain function and multiple intelligences that are beyond the scope of this book.[6] Suffice it to say that considering both intuitive and critical responses to a work of art will provide us with different paths to understanding, and one approach may be much more comfortable than another, depending on the individual.

In the simplest sense, reflection begins with noting a "gut reaction." However, careful contemplation takes more work: concentrated attention to the subject at hand. Jennifer A. Moon explains in *A Handbook of Reflective and Experiential Learning,* "... the content of reflection is largely what we know already. It is often a process of re-organizing knowledge and emotional orientations in order to achieve further insights" (82). In other words, reflection means not just seeing/hearing/sensing with a knee-jerk reaction, but contemplating how and why a play moves us and what it means to us in a personal way.[7] Contemplation and deep reflection helps us explore visceral reactions, interconnectivity, metaphor, and ultimately personal meaning.

When becoming acquainted with a script, the pondering mind is not concerned with Aristotle's classifications or Stanislavski's beats and units, but with encountering the play holistically and discovering personal reactions that deserve further probing. At first glance, the exercise below may seem deceptively simple, but contemplating *how and why* you responded viscerally makes the process more complex and personal. Carey Perloff, Artistic Director of the American Conservatory Theater, explains the value of probing the script from a personal perspective: "Directing is a completely intuitive art form. You read a script, and you meet it half way. Something in that script speaks to you. And you start to create. You start to see images. You start to see actors. You start to see patterns" (Fliotsos and Vierow 340).

EXERCISE: Reflective questions about the play

1. Record the following visceral responses with your first reading of the play, jotting notes in the margins when each occurs:
   - thoughts or reactions
   - feelings
   - ideas
   - images
   - sounds
   - smells
   - tactile responses

   Challenge yourself to find one of each of these responses, though some may be stronger than others. Do these responses change with subsequent readings? Explain.

2. What are your subjective responses to the play in terms of:
   - emotional response (e.g., joy, anxiety, anger, sadness)
   - physical response (e.g., tenseness, crying, laughing)
   - intellectual response (e.g., ideas and philosophies)
   - spiritual response (e.g., sense of connection to a creator or the universe – or, alternately, a world void of spirituality. Perhaps your own religious beliefs provoke a response to the play.)
   - other responses?

3. Further contemplation and personalization:

   Reflect on your responses and answers above. What is it about your personal experience or point of view that contributes to your reaction? For example, are there cultural mores, ethical values, personal experiences, memories, dreams, or other phenomena that come into play? Write a journal entry that explains and summarizes your reflection.

More contemplative practice: Zen as an interpretative lens

In a world full of constant distraction, our minds our constantly buzzing. How can we quiet the mind in order to prepare ourselves to tune into our visceral interpretations? One solution is the ancient practice of meditative breathing. You may have encountered breathing exercises in acting classes, yoga, or martial arts. In this case, we will examine the ideas and basic practice of centering meditation through Zen Buddhism.

Centering and meditative breathing are a means to creating a new awareness, or "mindfulness." Mindfulness is the opposite of mindlessness: things we do when our brain is on "autopilot" such as eating, brushing our teeth, or washing the dishes. Most of us either multitask or entertain a variety of random thoughts while doing routine tasks. (Where did I put my car keys? What should I have for lunch? I need to call the doctor.) To be mindful is to contemplate the action at hand, to create a new awareness of what is actually happening. In a world that prizes multitasking, it asks us to be in the moment, focusing deeply only on one task, even if that task is simple, such as the task of listening or reading. In *The Miracle of Mindfulness* Zen master Thich Nhat Hanh explains that when doing a routine task, such as washing the dishes, one should not let the mind wander, but focus solely on the task at hand. "At first glance, that might seem a little silly: why put so much stress on a simple thing? But that's precisely the point. ... I'm being completely myself, following my breath, conscious of my presence. There's no way I can be tossed around mindlessly like a bottle slapped here and there on the waves" (3–4).

Focused, concentrated attention is the product of meditation, or *zazen*, in the Zen tradition. Meditation allows the practitioner to focus on the breath and still the mind, dismissing hundreds of other daily distractions. By meditating routinely, you eventually come to a centered self – what is sometimes called "no-mind" – a state that invokes a different sense of reality than our day-to-day, surface reality.

It is important to realize that there is not one type of Zen, rather there are many varieties, deriving from Indian Buddhism that dates back some 1,500 years. Virtually all introductory books on Zen (and there are many) explain that Zen can never fully be intellectually understood; it is to be experienced.[8] Nonetheless, reading about Zen will help you understand how this "way of seeing" can be beneficial to artists and those interpreting art. Consider this not as a "method of script analysis" but as a way of understanding and contemplating life, and by extension, art. On a side note: just because you are trying meditation, which is integral to Buddhist practice, it should not threaten your own religious beliefs (or lack thereof); a number of world religions engage in meditative practice, as do many atheists.[9]

Zen has a connection to the arts through the creation of "Zen arts," such as poetry, painting, calligraphy, and flower arranging. In terms of theatre, Japanese Noh plays are based upon Zen principles and teachings. To the Western eye, a Noh performance progresses through a warped sense of time and aesthetics that are baffling, but upon study of Zen ideals, the beauty of the art form reveals itself. By stretching your mind outside of your "comfort zone" of linear thinking, you can enable yourself to see art and life from another perspective.

One way for Westerners to grasp the meaning of Zen is through Eugen Herrigel's now classic book, *Zen in the Art of Archery*. Herrigel, a German, writes of his travels in Japan and his attempt to master archery using Zen techniques, in essence to "be one with the arrow." He nearly gives up as he tries time and time again to trick his body or mind into making it appear as if the arrow could shoot itself rather than the archer shooting the arrow. He writes, "It is necessary for the archer to become, in spite of himself, an unmoved center. Then comes the supreme and ultimate miracle: art becomes 'artless,' shooting becomes not-shooting" (20). This mystical quality – the effort becoming effortless – is abundant in Zen texts and relates easily to art: the brush paints for itself, the photo selects itself, and the play writes itself. In terms of acting we call it being "in the moment;" for sports it is being "in the zone." In *The Essentials of Zen Buddhism*,

Zen priest Shunryu Suzuki writes, "The worst enemy of Zen experience, at least in the beginning, is the intellect, which consists and insists in discriminating subject from object" (293). To the Zen mind, subject and object become one. The artist is not simply transforming something into art, s/he is transformed *by* it as well.

Perhaps you have experienced such moments of clarity, in which all mental and physical effort seem suspended and artistry and creativity flow freely. But how can you reproduce this state? Although there is no quick or easy technique to "switch on" this state, meditation is the Zen pathway to seeing the world differently, a path that some Western artists have followed with great success. Initially, embracing a Zen philosophy means giving up a bit of yourself and your conception of everyday reality, – a difficult idea for some to accept. Zen identifies a constant state of change, without a single "fixed" reality; Zen also contemplates the nature of human suffering. To see through Zen eyes is to see the interrelated nature of a universe in constant flux. Zen master Shunryu Suzuki writes:

> Whatever we see is changing, losing its balance. The reason everything looks beautiful is because it is out of balance, but its background is always in perfect harmony…. So if you see things without realizing the background of Buddha nature, everything appears to be in the form of suffering. But if you understand the background of existence, you realize that suffering itself is how we live, and how we extend our life. (31–32)[10]

Contemplating the full meaning of Suzuki's statements requires some in-depth study of Zen. The issues and ideas are profound and metaphysical. They take time to grasp and require patience.

Zen and art

To increase our understanding of the connection between Zen and art, it is helpful to examine several visual artists who have transformed their view of art and the world through Zen. Author Jaquelynn Baas traces the influence of Zen on Western artists in her book *Smile of the Buddha*. Exploring the connection between Zen and artistic practice, she reasons:

> Art comes from and is realized in a place before language, outside of the discursive mind. It shares this place, the place of emptiness, with Buddhist meditation practice. This is one reason why a consideration of the relationship between art and Buddhism turns out to be so rewarding. (10)

Baas writes that Zen expression connotes "simple beauty that evokes a sense of the transience of life" (14). For example, a walk through a Zen garden produces constantly shifting perspectives, signifying a place that is not static, but in a constant state of change (Figure I.2). Baas explores the Zen art connection of many visual artists, though we focus on only a few here.

Both Wassily Kandinsky and Johannes Itten worked in and around the period of the First World War. When their normal and orderly worlds were shattered, Buddhist thinking helped them see the world in new and interesting ways. Kandinsky found his view of everyday reality fell apart as he contemplated the groundbreaking science of the atom during his lifetime; rather than a structured world of surface reality, he found "Everything became uncertain, precarious and insubstantial" (Kandinsky 363). No longer seeing the world dualistically – that is seeing a division of mind and matter – he wrote:[11]

> [Non-dualism] set me free and opened up new worlds for me. Everything "dead" trembled. Everything showed me its face, its innermost being, its secret soul, inclined more often to silence than to speech. ... This was enough for me to "comprehend," with my entire being and with all my senses, the possibility and existence of that art which today is called "abstract" as opposed to "objective." (Kandinsky 361)

Along with Kandinsky, Johannes Itten became one of the first professors (1919–1922) at the Bauhaus, a famous school of contemporary design in Weimar, Germany. Itten constructed a preliminary course for students, relying on nontraditional

Figure I.2   Zen rock garden

Source: Photo by Bud Coleman.

teaching methods, including gymnastics, improvisational song, and meditative breathing. These methods helped pave the way for creative work, "concentrating the students' spirits, which tend to become diffused" (Kaneko 99). In *Design and Form: The Basic Course at the Bauhaus and Later* (1975), Itten argues that an artist needs to see with an inner eye and to draw from inspiration. He reflects:

> To draw a large circle free-hand with a brush calls for complete body control and the greatest mental concentration. A famous Chinese ink drawing consists of a single circle painted on silk. Although the line of the circle is uniformly thin throughout, it yet reflects the artist's feeling. One of the most important principles of the Chinese painter is: "Heart and Hand must be One." (110)

Meditation has aided many artists in finding this inner resource. When performance artist Laurie Anderson discovered Zen meditation, it completely changed her perception. She explains, "When I open my eyes after a long meditation period, I suddenly seem to have about ten additional degrees of peripheral vision, like through a fisheye lens. The first time this happened, I felt like I was understanding space for the first time the way an architect might. It became pure volume" (Baas 201). She also discovered a new reality of time and of living in the moment (199). This altered perception of time and reality has led her to experiment with sound, music, story, and image in unorthodox ways and to delve into the world of dreams.

Likewise, experimental artist and musician John Cage was changed by Zen meditation and came to the conclusion that Zen art served a purpose: "to sober and quiet the mind so that it is in accord with what happens." Rather than letting our experiences be warped through our habits, our likes, and dislikes, Cage would have us see "...the flow of reality in all its richness. The purpose of art is to open our hearts and minds to the experience of that richness" (Baas 159).

EXERCISE: Zen and art

1. Discuss an experience of "no-mind," when you became one with your art. Perhaps you had a sense of a paint brush moving without thinking, or of performing seamlessly, – as if you had taken on a new life within a play. You may have had this sense in sports or some other arena as well. What do you think led you to this state, and were you able to recreate it? If you can't recall "no-mind" from your own experience, have you seen it in others? Explain.

2. Choose one of the following quotations and explain what it means to you by relating a personal experience of your own:

   Art is everywhere; it's only seeing which stops now and then. (John Cage, quoted in Baas 163)

   Technical knowledge is not enough. One must transcend techniques so that the art becomes an artless art, growing out of the unconscious. (D. T. Suzuki, quoted in Hyams 91)

   I don't think that art comes from art. A lot of artists apparently think so. I think it comes from the awakening person. (Isamu Noguchi, visual artist, quoted in Baas 113)

3. Conduct an image search online for "Zen art" and choose one image that intrigues you or that you connect to. Explain, as best you can, the beauty of this image and your connection to it. How does it embrace any of the ideas discussed above?

Tapping into intuition: breathe, read, reflect

As artists we realize the need to read the script multiple times to gain a complete understanding and working knowledge in preparation for production. Invariably, when we specialize, we train ourselves to read from a particular stance. For example, a costume designer may automatically search for period, season, character, socioeconomic status, etc., when reading. Some performers read scripts wondering which role is right for them, trying to identify with the characters. Although these questions are critical, save them for subsequent readings and put off production research until you have initially read the play from an open perspective. Your initial reading of the script should be an intuitive reaction to the world of the play, so read the entire script in one sitting, and try not to let your mind dissect the parts; instead, let the words, images, and other associations wash over you. Forget for a moment that you are a theatre artist and simply read the script as a human being. Let it work on you and engulf you. Try to dive into the world of the play and experience it from within.

Figure I.3   Meditative stance
Source: Photo by Anne Fliotsos.

In *The Zen of Creativity,* Zen Master John Daido Loori dedicates a chapter to responding to art intuitively and openly. He writes that though it is difficult to suspend judgment, the first step is to express feelings, not "ideas, criticisms, or opinions," a step which is exceedingly difficult for some people (104). To reflect on a performance piece or a reading he advises, "Stay aware of your visceral experience throughout. Allow yourself to become the music, words, or dance, noticing the sensations in your body. When the piece ends, close your eyes and intensify them" (106). In all of his exercises he emphasizes focus on the breath and relaxation in preparation for your response. In essence, you must clean your palate before tasting anything new.

Meditation before reading the script, especially if done on a regular basis, can help you come to the script with heightened attention and awareness. Although there are hundreds of styles of meditation, you need not study meditation in order to try it in its most simple form (see Exercise below).[12]

EXERCISE: Beginning meditation

1. Find a quiet place; turn off all phones and block interruptions.
2. Sit comfortably in a chair or on a cushion on the floor, but keep your spine in alignment, with a sense of lifting from the crown of your head (see Figure I.3). The back should not round or arch. If sitting on the floor you may cross your legs or sit in half or full lotus.
3. Place your hands comfortably on your legs or knees, palms up with thumb and middle finger touching, or try putting the hands in your lap palms up, one on top of the other with thumbs touching.
4. Bring your attention to the breath; begin breathing deeply and evenly, feeling the lower belly expand and contract in a natural cycle. Gradually slow and deepen the breath.
5. Focus on the breath, allowing your mind to clear. When thoughts come, acknowledge them, then let them go. Counting from one to ten in cycles (inhale one, exhale two,

> etc.) may help you focus. For some people, focusing on an
> image or repeating a mantra can be helpful.
> 6. Retain this posture and breathing for ten to fifteen minutes
>   the first time, building up to twenty or thirty minutes. Try
>   to do this daily, preferably in the morning and/or evening.

Adjusting to meditation

The first time you try meditation you will realize how much your
mind chatters and how difficult it is to regain control and still-
ness. You may find a virtual flood of thoughts (sometimes called
the waterfall) that is difficult to stop. Do not be discouraged.
Learning to meditate is a process, and it may take months before
you start to feel its deeper effects. Many beginners report that it
allows them to sleep better and to relieve stress fairly quickly, so
the benefits even at this level are worthwhile. Long-term effects
are even more rewarding. Recent studies show that people who
meditate regularly have enhanced immune systems and a more
positive outlook on life.[13] An excellent book to help you along the
many stages of developing your meditation is Sakyong Mipham's
Turning the Mind into an Ally (2003).

In his book *Psychophysical Acting* (2009), Phillip B. Zarrilli
describes exercises that focus on the breath and inner concentra-
tion/connectedness through yoga and martial arts, "cultivating
a certain type of awareness, attentiveness, and perception of the
bodymind-in-action and in relation to an environment" (29). I
summarize Philip Zarrilli's advice to the novice here: 1) not to
zone out, but to find a focused, energized concentration; 2) not
to expect a major spiritual encounter; 3) not to distract yourself
by working too hard, but to keep attention coming back to the
breath (29–30). In closing, Zarilli reminds students that the work
is for themselves, writing, "they must begin from the first day
to become their own teachers, that is, to internalize the disci-
pline…. Such attention to the focused and concentrated deploy-
ment of their (energized) bodies in space through time must
become intuitive" (30).

As the caveats above illuminate, pupils of meditation go
through a period of questioning and frustration. I've heard my
own students gripe, "I still don't see how breathing is going to

help me understand a play." It is not so simple, nor so direct a relationship. One of Zarrilli's students struggled at first, but eventually found her way, reflecting, "The idea of focusing the 'inner eye' on the breath made sense to me, but it wasn't as easy as I thought. ... At some point ... I finally gave up the 'trying,' and that's when I actually made some progress" (31). Much like the lesson in *Zen in the Art of Archery*, it takes time for the pupil to relax into the training and find the path. Once found, the arrow can begin to shoot itself.

As a final thought, consider the wisdom of Buddhist meditation master Chögyam Trungpa, who writes: "I would like to encourage everybody to practice meditation so we can actually see and look more. If we don't understand ourselves, it will be very difficult to appreciate anything else that goes on in our world. And on the whole, please cheer up. Don't analyze too much" (108).

EXERCISE: Breathe, read, reflect

Work on developing a practice of meditation before going on to this exercise, which is based in part on an exercise from Loori's book. Here we combine previous exercises into one practice.

Breathe

- Remove yourself from any distractions and turn off your phone. Sit upright and commit to deep, centered breathing, letting go of thoughts. Allow yourself to find a calm, centered state.

Read

- Suspend your critical and analytical reading for now and simply read the play straight through. Actors should resist the temptation to focus on character and designers the temptation to read for design clues.
- Focus your mind's eye on entering into the world of the play and going on the journey of the play from within, wherever and however it takes you. For example, if there is

a gunshot, imagine hearing/seeing/smelling it, feeling its vibrations and sensing the impact of that shot within the world.

- Notice your senses: sounds, images, colors, tactile or other sensations and associations; also note visceral feelings, such as a tight stomach, or a moment of elation.
- Note your responses as you read, jotting notes or symbols, and key words. You can also note fleeting associations to past experiences or other works of art or fiction. Do not stop to analyze at this point, just read and notate.

Reflect

- As you finish the play, close your eyes and return to your breathing. What sensations resonate the most? With what sense has the play left you? Review your list of initial responses and begin to question what provoked those responses. Go back to passages or descriptions that were particularly vivid and explore those sensations further.
- Next, write an informal, journal-type response of one to two pages that focuses on your initial sensations and free associations, suspending more analytical issues for the moment. The following questions may help you:

  Were you able to submerge yourself into the script, in terms of letting the script work on you? How so?

  How did your visceral responses change, and in response to what?

  What do you feel is the "heart" or central essence of the script?

  If you are disconnected from the play, what accounts for your lack of connection? What questions do you still have?

Though the questions in the exercise above are fairly general, further contemplation of your reactions may reveal some telling truths. *How* did the script engage you (if it did)? Were your reactions primarily intellectual, or where they more emotional, spiritual, or physical (a racing pulse, tenseness, or crying, for example)? What personal experiences or biases may color your reflection? Traumatic events such as incest in Paula Vogel's *How I Learned to Drive* or depression and suicide in Marsha Norman's *'Night Mother* may provoke extremely personal and volatile reactions based on our own experiences. Probing such issues may be difficult, but understanding your personal reaction to and connection with the script is vital.[14] Also consider what the script has to say about the human condition. Even the most serious scripts dealing with suffering and trauma can have a breath of optimism. Is there love? Hope? Humor? Compassion? Further readings will reveal new insights and pathways for exploration. If you were disconnected from the play, ask yourself why and try rereading it. At times we are overwhelmed in the first read, just trying to understand the world of the play and its path. Master teacher Trungpa explains, "Having *seen*, then you begin to *look* beyond that level and to develop a sense of composure about the whole thing. You actually begin to perceive how the world hangs together. If you want to design something or other, first you see the possibilities of the design; then you can begin to scrutinize and look further" (108).

Foregrounding the body as an interpretive tool

Breath is a part of the body-mind connection, but how else can the body contribute to our response to the text?

Playwright and professor Suzan Zeder argues that playwrights should free the body in order to free the creative mind, observing that "many writers tend to depend on the mind and ignore the body as they sit for hours at a time, staring at a page or computer screen, thinking that they are exercising only their fingers. ... A restricted, tightly bound, tense body does not allow for keen perception, expansive ideas, and the confidence necessary for creative work" (11–12). The same holds true for those of us who sit in a chair dissecting a script. We privilege the logical mind, divorcing it from any somatic intelligence. Studies in cognitive science support the body as a site of discovery.[15] Reviewing the literature of cognitive science and pedagogy, professor Paula

Leverage writes, "It has long been recognised that physical activity enhances mental activity. However, what is new is the recognition that cognition is embodied. We cannot think without our bodies, and this goes well beyond recognising that thought is a neurological, biological process" (11).

Interpreting through the body is a valid avenue of script exploration that is utilized by actors in rehearsal, but rarely used in an academic setting to study the script. Furthermore, when exploration through doing/enacting is utilized, it is often *after* an analytical examination of the text. What might happen if somatic interpretation were to come first? You may know of directors who like to postpone or cut table work to get a rehearsal "up on its feet." This "feetfirst" approach taps into performers' instincts, privileging intuitive body-mind-soul responses. Results can be unexpected and exciting, provoking new ways of thinking about the text and providing new contexts for understanding. In *The Inner Life of Asanas,* Swami Lalitanada writes:

> Through the movement of the body, we can observe the mind and emotions and make our thoughts tangible to ourselves. We can catch subtle glimmers and insights, hindrances and obstacles and write them down instead of letting them escape and vanish. ... The unconscious also comes up with some amazing symbolism that the conscious mind may not understand right away, or may not even want to admit. (18)

Although many theatre groups and directors have privileged somatic knowledge with their techniques, particularly experimentalists who de-emphasize text, few teachers incorporate the body into script interpretation. Several approaches are highlighted here to provide examples, including the Lookingglass Theatre's exploration through *tableau vivant* and Julie Taymor's use of ideograph.[16]

Chicago's Lookingglass Theatre, known for its devised works and adaptations, incorporates stunning visual iconography in performance. At the 2006 Conference of the Association of Theatre in Higher Education (ATHE) in Chicago, Lookingglass held a workshop on devising, which included the use of mobile sculpture, or *tableau vivant*, as a way of signifying meaning in storytelling. Although the emphasis was on devising, this method can be altered to help performers express ideas from the text by using their bodies in space, thus privileging the intuitive and provoking bodily-kinesthetic and spatial intelligences.[17] Such a launching point de-emphasizes spoken language and allows both the people enacting and observing the *tableau* to enter a world of visual metaphor and personal interpretation. The following technique, adapted from the Lookingglass exercise, provokes the exploration of a theme or motif in the text.

Figure I.4 Lookingglass Theatre workshop at DirectorsLabChicago
Source: Photo by Anita Evans.

EXERCISE: *Tableau vivant*

1. Form small groups (four people to a group works well) and choose a theme or motif from the text that you wish to investigate.
2. With little or no talking, each group member "sculpts" one image of the chosen concepts, using the other members as clay.
3. Next, sequence the images, transitioning from one to the next, and holding each for approximately three seconds. The sequence need not be in chronological order, and group members can come in and out of the sculpture as needed.
4. Present the sequence to other groups, asking for their interpretations before launching into the sculptor's ideas.

In my own use of the exercise above, we sculpted images of motherhood, which led to a discussion of motherhood in our own lives and ultimately in Lisa Loomer's play, *Living Out*. The discussion then extended to an investigation of the point of view about motherhood through the eyes of several characters in the play. The series of tableaux became an exciting site of discovery, exposing personal associations and experiences that we may not have otherwise shared.

A related exercise is the exploration of *ideograph*, a technique that director Julie Taymor employs, which she learned from movement expert Jacques Lecoq and experimentalist Herbert Blau. The word ideograph is derived from the Greek words for "idea" and "write" and can refer to a written symbol, such as a hieroglyphic, but can also be enacted. Taymor explains, "In the visual arts, an example of an ideograph would be a Japanese brush painting of a bamboo forest: just three or four quick brush strokes capture the whole. In the theatre, an ideograph is also a pared down form – a kinetic, abstract essence of an emotion, and action, or a character" (Taymor 139). Blau described the ideograph as a vortex; in action, the actor expresses "the kernel of each action without the distracting details" (Blumenthal and Taymor 12).[18]

In a television interview, Taymor explained ideograph by performing an extemporaneous ideograph of herself: she held her hands up to her face like blinders, slowly moved her hands forward toward a focal point, wrestled her hands together, then returned to a stance of composure, with her arms crossed over her chest (Bravo n.d.). Her metaphor as someone who ardently pursues a goal (the gesture of blinders and hands moving forward), wrestles with the creative process (the wringing of hands), and comes to closure (arms over chest) became amazingly clear without words.

Finding an ideograph for a particular character is one application of this method. This is a difficult work of synthesis and can complement analytical work on character, paring that work down. Search for a movement or gesture (or brief series thereof) that reveals the essence of a chosen character. Do not think literally of a character's gestures, but metaphorically, of expressing a central essence of the character. For example, an ideograph for the character of Antonio Salieri in Peter Shaffer's *Amadeus* might be self-flagellation. Throughout the play, Catholic composer Salieri tortures himself because he believes that despite his piety, God has deprived him of true genius and privileged Mozart in his place. The act of flagellation, or whipping oneself, was an act of penance in the medieval Catholic church, and serves as a metaphor for Salieri's punishment in God's eyes. Salieri does not literally whip himself in the play, but the metaphor of mental torture and the legacy of Catholic penance make this a strong ideograph for the actor, director, and designers.

Associational materials

Designers often feel more comfortable using image, sound, and artifact as means of expression, rather than enacting with their bodies. One technique used in production is the sharing of associational materials; often the director asks designers and cast members to bring pictures, music, or objects (including scents and tactile elements) that give them a sense of the play. These

materials need not be literal. In fact, abstract associations provoke interesting discussion and discoveries that may otherwise
never come to light. After your first reading of the play, review
your notes about your reactions. Perhaps you were reminded of
a particular movie, art work, artist, song, sound, object, smell,
taste, or texture. Explore that relationship to the text and bring
examples with you the next time your group meets to discuss
the text, explaining the connection you found. You may be
inspired by a mood or tone in the play. Do some searching. If
you are having a hard time getting started, the internet is an
excellent resource. Perhaps a word comes to mind first – oppres-
sion, suspense, rejuvenation – whatever it may be. Do an image
search on the internet to see what surfaces. Serendipity is often
your best friend as you search for associations. Keep an open
mind and an open heart and look for connections, even as
you are living your daily life. Inspiration can strike in unlikely
places.

A more specific investigation, which reflects the kernel of the
play, is to find an image or ideograph that could serve as the
poster for the play. Before you begin, search for poster designs on
a different play first, in order to examine how posters communicate the essence of a play. Note the wide variety: images may be
photos, collages, abstract art, or word-oriented images. For example, an image search on the internet for "Doll's House poster
Ibsen" produces a wide array of concepts, colors, and layouts that
arouse immediate responses. One is sexual, another starkly grim;
one invokes an image of servitude, another a broken doll. How
and why do these images speak to you? Color, image, line, composition, word choice, font, use of negative space – all of these
(and more) create impressions. How do they agree or disagree
with your own interpretation of the play? What do they lead you
to believe about the interpretations of the particular productions
they represent? After this preliminary study of posters, continue
on your own journey to communicate what you find to be the
essence of your play (at this point as a script rather than a real-
ized production). What do you have to say, and how can you best
convey it?

EXERCISE: Associations and central images

1. After exploring your visceral responses to the play, bring in associational materials to share with your class or production team. Challenge yourself to find at least three different types of associations, not relying merely on visual reference. Associational materials might include (but are not limited to):
   - Art work or photographs
   - A symbol
   - A scent (brought in a plastic bag, for example)
   - Music
   - Recorded or live sound
   - Textiles or other objects that can be felt
   - An object as artifact
   - Something to taste
2. What is the heart of the script, and what could serve as a central image for the play? Alone or with a collaborator, make a sketch of a poster design featuring the central image. It may be literal or abstract, but be prepared to explain how and why this image represents the play and might also reach a prospective audience. Indicate color and placement of any text, as well as font. How have you used negative space as well as positive to make the most visual impact on someone passing this poster? Before explaining the concept, let others in the group respond to the poster design. What grabs their attention?, What does it communicate to them?

Note that there is no single formula or method for the contemplation of a play text. As master acting teacher Robert Benedetti explains, "We do not teach rules and formulas but rather assist the student in developing richer perceptions and capacities. To do this well requires infinite patience and humility" (104). As you begin your contemplation of the text, the following summary of questions from this section will help you formulate your response. If you are writing a play response or journal entry, do not simply answer these questions in a rote manner, but use them to provoke your thinking before you write. Remember, too, that subsequent readings of the play will trigger additional reactions, so stay attuned.

Questions for application

- What are your visceral responses with your first reading of the play? Include thoughts, feelings, ideas, images, sounds, smells, and tactile responses.
- What are your subjective responses to the play in terms of emotional, physical, intellectual, and spiritual responses?
- Do your visceral and subjective responses change with subsequent readings? Explain.
- What is it about your personal experience or point of view that contributes to your reaction? For example, are there cultural mores, ethical values, personal experiences, memories, dreams, or other phenomena that come into play?
- Were you able to submerge yourself into the script, in terms of letting the script work on you, or were you removed from it? Explain.
- If you were not engaged in the script, what stood in your way?
- How might a major idea in the play be expressed nonverbally (image, sculpture, sound, music, textile, object, scent, etc.)?
- What do you feel is the "heart" of the script? How might the kernel of the play be expressed as an ideograph (either as a written symbol or performed pose, or linked poses)?
- How might one character be expressed as an ideograph?
- How might the play be expressed visually and metaphorically, as a production poster? What does that poster communicate, and how?
- What questions do you still have about the script and your relation to it?

Notes

1. For more information, see Richard Hooker's website, "Chinese Philosophy: Yin and Yang" Washington State University, 1996 [cited July 2, 2008], http://www.wsu.edu/~dee/CHPHIL/YINYANG.HTM.
2. Some of Wilson's productions have lasted through the night and into the next day; others juxtaposed the extraordinarily slow motions of performers with fast motion. These are only two examples of many. For information on Wilson and photographs of his striking visual design, see the Robert Wilson homepage, http://www.robertwilson.com.
3. *Prana* may be translated as breath or vital life force, similar to the notion of *qi* in Chinese culture (*ki* in Japanese), though *qi* is less concrete. Zarrilli explains that *qi* is "neither matter nor energy, but rather 'matter on the verge of becoming energy' (Kaptchuk 1983, 35). ... *Qi* animates all movement..." (74).
4. See Sharon M. Carnicke's *Stanislavski in Focus* and recent translations of Stanislavski by Jean Benedetti.
5. In addition, social scientists might call this subjective quest a phenomenological approach. Phenomenology is the study of phenomena placed within the context of first person, human experience. According to *The Stanford Encyclopedia of Philosophy*, "The central structure of an experience is its intentionality, its being directed toward something, as it is an experience of or about some object" (Smith n.p.). A similar idea is reflected in constructivist education, which stems in part from theories proposed by Dewey, Jean Piaget, and others. The constructivist premise is simple: knowledge does not exist as some absolute truth to be learned; instead, the learner must construct his or her own meaning.

    Phenomenological and constructivist principles are relevant when we consider the telling or hearing of a story, which has many possible realms of interpretation based on what we bring of ourselves.
6. Further studies on intelligence include Raymond B. Cattell's distinction between fluid and crystallized intelligence, Howard Gardner's work on multiple intelligences and Mihaly Csikszentmihalyi's research on art and "flow." For a discussion of further right and left-brain studies, see also John McCrone's "'Right Brain' or 'Left Brain'–Myth Or Reality?" [cited February 20, 2008] for *New Scientist* at http://www.rense.com/general2/rb.htm.
7. Calling for such personal reactions juxtaposes with the tradition of Western pedagogy: to respond in an objective, analytical manner.

Educational theorist Philip Taylor writes that people may at first be put off by reflective writing, thinking it insinuates self-absorption. He refutes this view, arguing, "On the contrary, the reflective practitioner stance demands a discovery of self, a recognition of how one interacts with others, and how others read and are read by this interaction. It is a stance particularly neglected.... [F]or arts educators to ignore reflective practitioner design is to remain ignorant to the kind of artistic processes which are the lifeblood of our work" (Taylor 27).

8. In *Zen Buddhism: Selected Writings of D. T. Suzuki*, editor William Barrett cautions, "Zen Buddhism presents a surface so bizarre and irrational, yet so colorful and striking, that some Westerners who approach it for the first time fail to make sense of it, while others, attracted by this surface, take it up in a purely frivolous and superficial spirit. Either response would be unfortunate" (Suzuki vi).

9. For information on Hindu meditation, see www. project-meditation.org; for Christian meditation, see the World Community of Christian Meditation website; for Jewish meditation, see the Iyyun website. Atheists also practice meditation for its benefits, for meditation does not rely on a belief in a deity.

10. In a journal report entitled "Culture and Point of View," Richard E. Nesbitt and Takahiko Masuda report that on a study that has some relevance to Suzuki's statement about foreground and background. In one section of the study, they asked both Westerners and Japanese to photograph a subject. The majority of Westerners focused in closely on the subject at hand, providing little of the space around the subject, whereas the Japanese took their shots with a wide frame, including much of the surrounding environment and making the central object smaller, and a part of the environment. The study points to cognitive and aesthetic differences between East and West, particularly in terms of subject to field. [cited November 3, 2007], http://www.pnas.org/cgi/doi/10.1073/pnas.1934527100.

11. Dualism has various meanings, such as the opposite forces of good and evil. In the philosophy of the mind, dualism distinguishes opposites of mind and matter (mental/physical). Howard Robinson writes in *The Stanford Encyclopedia of Philosophy*, "common sense tells us that there are physical bodies, and... there is intellectual pressure towards producing a unified view of the world." Kandinsky reacts to the disintegration of this fixed view of a unified world and a new understanding about the interrelationship of the mental and physical.

12. Meditation may be done walking or lying down as well as sitting. Some students prefer mantras or guided meditations. Others prefer to join meditation groups, some of which are conducted through churches as "centering prayer." The internet, books, tapes and podcasts all offer many opportunities to learn more about meditative styles.

13. See the report on the Wisconsin-Madison study: "University study shows impact of meditation on brain, anti-bodies" by Katherine Combes [cited April 4, 2004]. Http:// Asianresearch.org/articles. A related study on meditating monks' brains searches for a link between their happiness and physiological changes in the brain. See "Monks help scientists study brain," BBC News world edition [cited September 26, 2003]. Http://news.bbc.co.uk/2/hi/south_asia/3142874.stm.

14. Physical and psychological trauma should not be taken lightly. If a script recalls a personal crisis, it is your responsibility to seek help and to notify your director or teacher of the problem at hand.

15. Studying the link between cognitive science and aesthetic judgment in visual art, Michael J. Parsons found that aesthetic judgment developed through five stages in children. The first stage is valuing the beauty of pictorial realism. More complex appreciations follow: "[T]hey gradually learn to appreciate representation, expression, and organization. Finally...the adult viewer learns to go beyond any existing criteria of appreciation and adopts an open-ended receptive attitude that allows him or her to respond to qualities of the work not yet encompassed in evaluation" (Csikszentmihalyi and Robinson 11). Mihaly Csikszentmihalyi and Rick E. Robinson also report that cognitive studies have been found somewhat lacking; German philosopher Alexander Gottlieb Baumgarten and his followers "separate[d] aesthetics from reason – [based on] the observation that the aesthetic experience provides visceral, holistic, and greatly rewarding sensations that are ordinarily absent from purely cognitive activities" (12).

16. The following sections on the Lookingglass Theatre and Julie Taymor are previously published or adapted from my article, "From Script Analysis to Script Interpretation: Valorizing the Intuitive." *Theatre Topics* 19.2 (September 2009): 153–63.

17. Howard Gardner, Professor in Cognition and Education at the Harvard Graduate School of Education, has been writing on his theory of Multiple Intelligences (MI) since his landmark book, *Frames of Mind,* in 1983. Among the eight intelligences available to

us are kinesthetic-bodily intelligence (high in dances and actors, for example) and spatial intelligence (high in architects and cartographers, for example). For further information on MI and pedagogy, see also Gardner's *Multiple Intelligences: New Horizons*.
18. Director Joanne Akalaitis takes a somewhat similar approach, though she refers to the gestural movements as *mudras*, a concept derived from the Indian Kathakali theatre. Michael Chekhov's work with psychological gesture and Stanislavski's work with physical action are related concepts, though the gestures they employ are geared more specifically to building characters than to illuminating the play in a more universal manner. Note the parallel to Meyerhold's conception of movement as he writes about biomechanics: "Every movement is a hieroglyph with its own peculiar meaning" (200).

Sources and further study

Akalaitis, Joanne. Interview with Arthur Bartow. In *The Director's Voice: Twenty-One Interviews*. New York: TCG, 1988, 3–19.

Angelo, Thomas A. and Patricia K. Cross. *Classroom Assessment Techniques: A Handbook for College Teachers*. 2nd ed. San Francisco: Jossey-Bass, 1993.

Baas, Jaquelynn. *Smile of the Buddha: Eastern Philosophy and Western Art from Monet to Today*. Berkeley, CA: University of California Press, 2005.

Barba, Eugenio. *The Dilated Body*. Rome: Zeami Libri, 1985.

Benedetti, Robert. "Zen and the Art of Actor Training." *Master Teachers of Theatre*. Ed. Burnet M. Hobgood. Carbondale, IL: Southern Illinois University Press, 1988, 85–105.

Blumenthal, Eileen and Julie Taymor. *Julie Taymor: Playing with Fire*. 2nd ed. New York: Abrams, 1999.

Bravo. *Bravo Profiles: Julie Taymor*. Unpublished videotape.

Cage, John. *Silence: Lectures and Writings*. Middletown, CT: Wesleyan University Press, 1961.

Carnicke, Sharon M. *Stanislavski in Focus*. 1st ed. London: Hardwood Academic, 1998; 2nd ed. published by London: Routledge, 2008.

Csikszentmihalyi, Mihaly and Rick E. Robinson. *The Art of Seeing: An Interpretation of the Aesthetic Encounter*. Malibu, CA: Getty Museum, 1990.

Dewey, John. *How We Think: A Restatement of the Relation of Reflective Thinking to the Educative Process*. Lexington: Heath, 1960 [1910].

Field, Richard. "John Dewey (1859–1952)." *Internet Encyclopedia of Philosophy.* Ed. James Fieser and Bradley Dowden, 2007. <http://www.iep.utm.edu/d/dewey.htm>. Cited October 21, 2008.

Fliotsos, Anne. "From Script Analysis to Script Interpretation: Valorizing the Intuitive." *Theatre Topics,* 19.2 (September 2009): 153–63.

Fliotsos, Anne and Wendy Vierow. *American Women Stage Directors of the Twentieth Century.* Urbana, IL: University of Illinois Press, 2008.

Fuchs, Elinor. "EF's Visit to a Small Planet: Some Questions to Ask a Play." *Theater,* 32.4 (Summer 2004): 5–9.

Gardner, Howard. *Frames of Mind: The Theory of Multiple Intelligences.* New York: Basic Books, 1983.

——. *Multiple Intelligences: New Horizons.* New York: Basic Books, 2006.

George, David E. R. *Buddhism as/in Performance: Analysis of Meditation and Theatrical Practice.* New Delhi: D. K. Printworld, 1999.

Herrigel, Eugen. *Zen in the Art of Archery.* New York: Vintage Books, 1999.

Hyams, Joe. *Zen in the World of Martial Arts.* New York: Bantam Books, 1982.

Itten, Johannes. *Design and Form: The Basic Course at the Bauhaus and Later.* New York: Van Nostrand Reinhold, 1975.

Kandinsky, Wassily. *Kandinsky: Complete Writings on Art.* New York: Da Capo Press, 1994.

Kaneko, Yoshimasa. "Japanese Painting and Johannes Itten's Art Education." *Journal of Aesthetic Education* 37.4 (Winter 2003): 93–101.

Kaptchuk, Ted J. *The Web That Has No Weaver: Understanding Chinese Medicine.* New York: Congdon and Weed, 1983.

Lalitananda, Swami. *The Inner Life of Asanas.* Ed. Kendra Ward. Kootenay, BC: Timeless Books, 2007.

Leverage, Paula. "Developing Cognitive Approaches to Literature, Film and Pedagogy: An Evolutionary Perspective." Presentation for the Center for Undergraduate Instructional Excellence (CUIE). Purdue University, West Lafayette, IN. March 24, 2009.

Loori, John Daido. *The Zen of Creativity: Cultivating Your Artistic Life.* New York: Ballantine Books, 2004.

Meyerhold, Vsevolod. *Meyerhold on Theatre.* Ed. and trans. Edward Braun. New York: Hill and Wang, 1969.

Mirriam-Webster Online. <www.mirriam-webster.com>. Cited March 11, 2009.

Moon, Jennifer A. *A Handbook of Reflective and Experiential Learning: Theory and Practice.* London: Routledge Falmer, 2004.

Nhat Hahn, Thich. *The Miracle of Mindfulness: A Manual on Meditation.* Boston, MA: Beacon Press, 1999.

Olf, Julian M. "Reading the Dramatic Text for Production." *Theatre Topics*, 7.2 (September 1997): 153–69.

O'Reilley, Mary Rose. *The Peaceable Classroom*. Portsmouth, NH: Heinemann, 1993.

Proehl, Geoffrey S. et al. *Toward a Dramaturgical Sensibility*. Madison, NJ: Fairleigh Dickinson University Press, 2008.

Robinson, Howard. "Dualism." *Stanford Encyclopedia of Philosophy*. Ed. Edward N. Zalta, 2003, <http://plato.stanford.edu/archives/fall2009/entries/dualism/> Cited October 17, 2007.

Smith, David Woodruff. "Phenomenology." *Stanford Encyclopedia of Philosophy*. Ed. Edward N. Zalta, 2003, <http://plato.stanford.edu/archives/win2005/entries/phenomenology/> Cited October 22, 2008.

Suzuki, Daisetz Teitaro. *Zen Buddhism: Selected Writings by D.T. Suzuki*. Ed. William Barrett. New York: Doubleday, 1996.

Suzuki, Shunryu. *Zen Mind, Beginner's Mind: Informal Talks on Zen Meditation and Practice*. New York: Weatherhill, 1999.

Taylor, Philip. "Introduction: Rebellion, Reflective Turning and Arts Education Research." *Researching Drama and Arts Education: Paradigms and Possibilities*. Ed. Philip Taylor. London: Routledge Falmer, 1996: 1–21.

Taymor, Julie with Alexis Greene. *The Lion King: Pride Rock on Broadway*. New York: Hyperion, 1997.

Trungpa, Chögyam and Judith L. Lief. *Dharma Art*. Boston, MA: Shambhala, 1996.

Wegner, William H. "The Creative Circle: Stanislavski and Yoga." *Educational Theatre Journal* 28.1 (March 1976): 85–89.

Wilson, Robert. Home page, <http://www.robertwilson.com> Cited June 23, 2009.

Zarilli, Phillip B. *Psychophysical Acting: An Intercultural Approach after Stanislavski*. London: Routledge, 2009.

Zeder, Suzan with Jim Hancock. *Spaces of Creation: The Creative Process of Playwriting*. Portsmouth, NH: Heinemann, 2005.

II

Formalist Analysis

Formalist analysis: an introduction

A close study of the script itself, as opposed to any type of contextual study (historical, sociopolitical, biographical, etc.) is sometimes referred to as formalist analysis. In his book *Script Analysis for Actors, Directors and Designers,* James Thomas describes formalist analysis as "the search for playable dramatic values that reveal a central unifying pattern that informs or shapes a play from the inside and coordinates all its parts" (xxi).[1] In other words, a close study of the components of the script and the structure of those components will ultimately reveal the script's playable values. It is upon Aristotle that we usually base a formalist approach, for he has provided classifications that allow us to systematically analyze a play, though this type of analysis works more readily with causal/linear plays rather than episodic, modernist, and postmodern works. Examples in the section on Aristotle below are taken mainly from Sophocles' *Oedipus the King* and Ibsen's *A Doll's House.* If you are unfamiliar with these plays, you are advised to read them before proceeding with this part of the book.

Aristotle: then and now

Aristotle, a revered teacher and philosopher of the fourth century BCE, wrote the first extant treatise on theatre criticism in the western world, the *Poetics,* reflecting on much of the golden age of Greek drama from the previous century. Scholars believe the *Poetics* was written as two books: one on tragedy and one on comedy, the second of which has been lost. Remarkably, the *Poetics* continues to be a foundational text in the analysis of drama some 2,400 years later, though it has also sparked debate. Over the centuries Aristotle's *Poetics* has been interpreted by artists and critics in a variety of ways, at times skewing his original ideas or taking them out of context. During the European Renaissance, for example, Aristotle's ideas were interpreted through the writings of the Roman philosopher Horace. During the French Renaissance, neoclassicists of the French Academy codified "rules" for writers based on Aristotle via Horace, though Aristotle himself never prescribed rules *per se.* In the *Poetics,* his prime objective was to observe and classify dramatic literature in a manner similar to the classification of genus and species in animal and plant life. (Biology and zoology were among Aristotle's many areas of scientific research, and classification was a part of his study of the natural world.)

Implicit in Aristotle's writing are biases based on Greek culture of the time, a culture which viewed women and slaves as having less worth, or at best different purposes, than Greek-born male citizens. Despite the cultural differences reflected in the drama, we can borrow from Aristotle's classification system and definitions, applying these concepts to our understanding of Greek drama and retooling some of his statements to fit more contemporary plays. Aristotle's tools remain useful, but should not be considered out of the context for which they were originally written, particularly in terms of value judgments of "good" or "bad" practices of play construction. For example, Aristotle held that the episodic plot was of lesser quality than the causal (linear) plot, a concept we no longer embrace in modern theatre.

Aristotle revealed: breaking down the *Poetics*[2]

The first step in any study of Aristotle is to read his actual text. At first read, the *Poetics* seems disjointed; some scholars believe it was written as a series of lectures or lecture notes. Increasing the difficulty, Aristotle references literature that is now obscure or can no longer be accessed. Although these sections are baffling, they are also interspersed with references to plays we know from Aeschylus, Sophocles, Euripides, and Aristophanes, giving us a more solid footing. Familiarity with Greek tragedy, particularly *Oedipus the King*, will be of great benefit to anyone studying the *Poetics*, for Aristotle holds up Sophocles' play as an example of excellence.

It is worthwhile to consult more than one translation and note how the structure of the *Poetics* varies slightly from one to another. Several older translations are available on the internet through the Library of Congress and Project Gutenberg, though readers may prefer a more modern translation, with notes and/or commentary. Some editions create numbered "chapters" of the original sections of text while others break down each section with titles based on theme, for ease of use. Here I reference two translations, by scholars Kenneth McLeish and Gerald F. Else. Use the quotations below as a study guide to the major concepts in Aristotle's *Poetics*, but not as a substitute for reading the text itself, which provides much more depth and context.

Aristotle begins in a scientific mode, by defining his terms and examining the relationships and distinctions among various types of poetry. He writes that a chief characteristic of all poetry (which includes drama) is the imitation of life through the portrayal of actions. He further clarifies that the characters performing the actions must be morally good or bad, and that characters in tragedy are "serious-minded," whereas those in comedy can be more ridiculous.

Key concepts and terms from this first section of the *Poetics* are identified below, followed by quotations from a translation of the *Poetics*:

Imitation: The chief purpose of all composition – epic, tragedy, comedy, dithyramb, the majority of instrumental music for flute or lyre – is the imitation (*mimesis*) of reality. (McLeish 3)

Action: Imitations are made of actions. The people doing or suffering these actions must be "good" or "bad" – the standard moral distinction between members of the human race. (McLeish 4)

Genre (origins): Serious-minded creators imitated "elevated" actions and the "elevated" characters who performed them. Less serious-minded creators imitated the actions of the less "elevated" characters, turning to satire as naturally as their serious colleagues turned to choral hymns.[3] (McLeish 6)

Comedy: When I say that comedy is the imitation of people "worse" than the average, this implied not total moral degeneracy but a falling from the ideal into one single form of such degeneracy, the ridiculous. The ridiculous can be defined as a mistake or a lapse from "perfection" which causes no pain or serious harm to others. (McLeish 8)

Epic poetry and tragedy: Epic is in narrative style and uses the same verse metre throughout, and its action has no fixed time-span, while that of tragedy is normally a single twenty-four hour period, or just over. (McLeish 9)

Next, Aristotle examines tragedy, again by dissecting the parts and describing the components that comprise this genre. He subsequently describes each component in further detail, but first he presents a concise description:

Tragedy, then, is a process of imitating an action which has serious implications, is complete [has a beginning, middle, and end], and possesses magnitude; by means of language which has been made sensuously attractive, with each of it's varieties found separately in the parts; enacted by the persons themselves and not presented through narrative; through a course of pity and fear completing the purification [*catharsis*] of tragic acts which have those emotional characteristics. (Else 25)

Today we still identify these as components of classical tragedy, though components of modern tragedy often differ. For example, Greek tragedy was written in verse, and the language of the play was to have a serious and elevated stature, for it represented the language of a noble hero. However, more modern dramas and tragedies, such as Arthur Miller's *Death of a Salesman*, present not a classical hero, but what some call an "antihero." Willy Loman is not a lofty character, but a downtrodden salesman.

One could argue that his morals are not high, nor is his language anything other than middle-class. Furthermore, Aristotle dictates that tragedy is presented through dialogue and not through narrative, though modern dramas may include narrative mixed with dialogue. For example in *To Kill a Mockingbird*, Christopher Sergel's dramatic adaptation of Harper Lee's novel, Scout narrates the story to the audience, then steps into the dialogue as a character, alternating between character and narrator throughout the play. Though dramatists have chosen to break with the classical form and find new options, some of Aristotle's principles have held true. For example, although Shakespeare adds the comic gravediggers scene into the tragic scenes of *Hamlet*, the main action of the play remains of "utmost seriousness," as are the consequences of the play.

Aristotle's attention to the seriousness of the action leads directly to his causal observation that tragedy moves one through pity and fear to a state of *catharsis*, or purging of emotion. He writes: "[T]he plot must be so structured even without benefit of any visual effect, that the one who is hearing the events unroll shudders with fear and feels pity at what happens: which is what one would experience on hearing the plot of *Oedipus*" (Else 40). The end product of tragedy, then, is to identify, confront, and purge the fears or repressed emotions of the human psyche; it is a process of cleansing.

After defining tragedy and its relationship to other poetic forms, Aristotle systematically identifies six elements of tragedy, each of which are intertwined. He also places value on these elements, naming plot as the most important element. Aristotle writes: [T]he structure of events, the plot, is the goal of tragedy, and the goal is the greatest thing of all" (Else 27). He lists the next five elements in order of importance: character, language, thought, the visual, and music. Aristotle observes, "These are the ingredients of tragedy, used by practically all dramatists; there are no others" (McLeish 10).

It follows that Aristotle must analyze the parts of the plot, beginning with the conception of wholeness, that is, having a beginning, middle, and end. The ordering of events is also of utmost importance; he writes that "the component events ought to be so firmly compacted that if any one of them is shifted to another place, or removed, the whole is loosened up and dislocated ... " (Else 32). His emphasis on the correct order of the events in the plot leads him to a judgment that causal (linear) plots are superior to episodic plots. In a causal plot, one event triggers the next, releasing a chain of events that lead to a crisis point and eventual resolution. However, in an episodic plot, episodes focusing on a common theme are loosely related rather than causal. It is possible, in some plays, that the scenes could be rearranged without distracting from the play's message. Aristotle writes: "Among simple plots and actions the episodic are the worst. By 'episodic' plot I mean one in which there is no probability or necessity for the order in which the episodes follow one another" (Else 34). Again, in modern times Aristotle's predilection for linear/causal plots is no longer common. Many well-regarded plays and films employ an episodic structure, either exploring theme through a variety of motifs or through different characters' perspectives. (We will consider examples of episodic plots later in this section.)

Aristotle continues his description of plot by elucidating the chief turning points in a tragedy. Both reversal and recognition (also called discovery) are hallmarks of Sophocles' *Oedipus the King*, Aristotle's primary example. *Reversal* is sometimes translated from the Greek as *peripety* or *peripeteia*. Aristotle writes, " 'Peripety' is a shift of what is being undertaken to the opposite ... " (Else 35–36). This can mean a sudden change of fortune, a change of circumstance, or a change of direction in the dramatic action. Aristotle describes *recognition,* often called *discovery* (or in Greek, *anagonorisis*) as "a change from ignorance to knowledge" (McLeish 15). In other words, a key piece of information is discovered or recognized. Later in the *Poetics*, he differentiates different types of recognition or discovery: "Discovery by marks or physical objects; ... contrived by the author; ... by memory, from deduction; ... through false deduction by the audience; ... and from the events themselves" (McLeish 22–24). Furthermore, Aristotle writes, "The finest recognition [discovery] is the one that happens at the same time as a peripety [reversal], as is the case with the one in the *Oedipus*" (Else 36). Later, he continues,

"The best recognition of all is one that arises from the events themselves; the emotional shock of surprise is then based on probabilities" (Else 47). For example, as Oedipus pursues the clues that will lead Thebes out of the plague, he *discovers* that he has killed his own father and married his mother. This *recognition* leads to his *reversal* of fortune and to a *reversal* of the action of the play. No longer is Oedipus the seeker and the hero, but the cause of the plague. The *catharsis*, or cleansing is three-fold: Oedipus purges his own emotion, gouging out his eyes; the audience purges its emotion, moved to pity and fear; and Thebes purges the foul cause of the plague (Oedipus), restoring the city to balance.

Aristotle also identifies two types of tragic plots, simple and complex, based on playwrights' use of recognition and reversal. He states: "By 'simple' action I mean one the development of which being continuous and unified in the manner stated above, the reversal comes without peripety or recognition, and by 'complex' action one in which the reversal is continuous but with recognition or peripety or both" (Else 35). Here Aristotle makes a further judgment, writing that "the construction of the finest tragedy should be not simple but complex, and at the same time imitative of fearful and pitiable happenings...." (Else 37–38). In short, he believes the best tragic plots combine recognition and reversal, which in turn lead to catharsis.

Finally, Aristotle turns to character, giving us his observations on the tragic hero. He points out that while the hero is of good character, he is also capable of making an error in judgment, the human factor to which we all relate. Aristotle observes, "They are not saints, but their sufferings are caused less by innate wickedness than because of *hamartia* ('error'). Heroes should be people of high degree and reputation" (McLeish 17). McLeish adds his own qualification, explaining in the translation that *"[h]amartia* is the failing in understanding or moral character which leads someone to a disastrous choice of action: a choice which arouses our pity because it is both catastrophic and made deliberately but not out of wickedness, and arouses our terror because we identify with both the innocence and the help-lessness of the person who makes the choice" (17). In further defining the essence of tragic characters, Aristotle writes, "First and most important, they must be 'good.' ... Second, character should be appropriate. ... Third, characters should fit their 'reality.' ... Fourth, character should be consistent" (McLeish 20–21). Here Aristotle reflects what we often call *decorum* for a character, reflecting that which is proper and congruous with the character's station and environment.

EXERCISE: Identifying Aristotelian elements

After reading a tragedy or serious drama, answer the following questions:

1. Refer back to Aristotle's definition of tragedy. How does the play you read compare with Aristotle's definition in terms of seriousness? Do the main characters' actions lead to catharsis? Explain.
2. Does your play have a distinct beginning, middle, and end? If so, explain where you would divide these larger parts of the plot and why at these junctions.
3. As Aristotle writes, "by 'episodic' plot I mean one in which there is no probability or necessity for the order in which the episodes follow one another" (Else 34). Is the play linear/causal, episodic, or some combination of the two? Justify your answer, looking at the relationship between scenes throughout the play.
4. Does the plot include both reversal and recognition? If so, explain at what points in the plot. Identify what type of discovery is made and whether, based on Aristotle's definition, the plot is simple or complex.
5. Is there a tragic hero of high character and reputation? What is his/her error in judgment (*hamartia*)? Does the character fit his/her reality (showing appropriate decorum), and remain consistent?
6. After considering the aspects above, do you consider the play a classical tragedy, a modern tragedy, or some other genre? Explain.

Application of formalist principles

Though Aristotle provided a starting point for analysis, further terminology and analytical systems have evolved over the centuries. In 1863, a German artist and scholar named Gustav Freytag wrote *Technik des Dramas,* giving us "Freytag's Pyramid" (see Figure II.1), a graphic depiction of the play's action with a central climax, which has been taught – at times in an altered form – for more than a century.

In his introduction to *Script Analysis for Actors, Directors and Designers,* Thomas points to Russian scholar and critic Alexander Veselovsky as an important source of dramatic analysis in the twentieth century. Veselovsky's ideas influenced Russian artists such as Mikhail Shchepkin, Vladimir Nemirovitch-Dantchenko, and Konstantin Stanislavski, among others, and those artists added their own interpretations as well (xxiii). In essence, what we now consider "traditional" script analysis is a composite of many artists' interpretations, and therefore the terminology and definitions of those terms do not always match – a vexing problem.

As we know, Aristotle's first and most important element is plot, which is not to be confused with story. Whereas a story tells

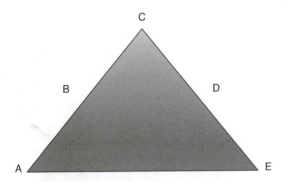

Figure II.1   Freytag's Pyramid of a causal/linear plot

Note: A) introduction, B) rise, C) climax, D) return or fall, E) catastrophe (Freytag 115)

Source: Freytag ([1863] 1968: 115).

what happens to a person (or group) from beginning to end, the plot is the structure of events within the play itself. Parts of the larger "story" exist outside of the plot and are only referenced in the plot as background or exposition. For example, in the play *A Doll's House,* we discover that Nora has forged a document to save her husband. Her actual forgery is not enacted in the play, but revealed as part of the background story. Think of the plot as a map or blueprint of the play itself, revealing its structure. How does this play unfold, and what links one scene to the next?

Actors and directors often use Stanislavski's terms "spine" or "through-line" to describe the *dramatic action* of a play. Dramatic action is not physical motion; it is the broader action of a character trying to resolve a conflict. For example, in *A Doll's House,* Nora covers up her past forgery in hopes of saving the couple's reputation. This cover-up is a crucial part of the dramatic action of the play. (Action is again addressed in a later section; see Stanislavski and the actor's script)

Based on Aristotle's elements, the following terms are common in formalist analysis, though not every term is found in Aristotle. Bear in mind that this type of analysis works best for causal/linear plays, especially in terms of the analysis of plot (Figure II.2). Where alternate terms are often used synonymously, they are noted.

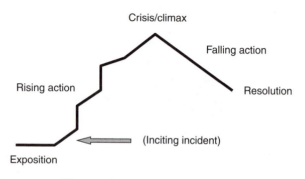

Figure II.2   Causal/linear plot

Plot (Causal/linear)

Exposition: introduces the audience (or reader) to the *world of the play* and to any background information required to begin the journey. The world of the play includes a wealth of vital information about the temporal and geographical setting, the characters and their relationships, the socioeconomic environment, the political climate, the level of education, and the state of balance or imbalance at the start of the play. As an example of imbalance, the play *Oedipus the King* opens amidst a plague in Thebes, a state of tremendous suffering for the city. Most tragedies open with a state of imbalance which calls for change; look for this in the exposition and compare it with the end of the play to see how the equilibrium has changed. For example, in *A Doll's House*, we discover in the first scene that Nora wants more money from Torvald; he chastises her for her spending and tells her to be more frugal. Though the conflict is slight and their marriage seems happy on the surface, this underlying imbalance foreshadows more serious conflicts in the play. What are the consequences by the play's end? Nora must leave her home in order for balance to be restored.

Though a wealth of vital exposition is given at the start of the play, some information is deliberately withheld by the playwright, allowing for *discoveries* later in the play, which trigger new choices and further the dramatic action. To build suspense, the playwright may withhold one crucial piece of the puzzle: a discovery of such importance that it triggers the major crisis of the play. In *Oedipus the King*, this discovery is that Oedipus has killed his father and married his mother. When studying exposition, examine how and when the playwright reveals exposition as well as how much is revealed or withheld.

Inciting Incident (or *Inciting Action*): the first major event that triggers a response, setting the rising action (or complication) into motion and leading to the major dramatic action or question of the play. In *A Doll's House* the inciting incident is Krogstad's arrival and his threat to blackmail Nora; she must take action in order to hide her secret from Torvald. In *Oedipus the King*, it is Oedipus' vow to rid Thebes of the plague that sets him on the path to his own downfall. Note that the inciting incident must occur within the plot itself, not before the play starts. Important events that occur before the curtain opens are part of the background story, revealed through the exposition. For example, at the start of Euripides' *Medea*, we learn that Medea's husband has agreed to marry another woman, triggering her rage, but because this happens before the play actually begins, it cannot be the inciting action of the plot.

Rising Action (or *Complication*): a series of small or moderate crises (complications) that push the action forward, building it to a peak. For example, in *A Doll's House*, Nora gets caught up in her lies to her husband, Torvald, and falls behind in her payments to the blackmailer, Krogstad, causing her to be further entangled in a series of small crises to cover her path of deception.

Crisis: the peak of the rising action at which the action of the play dramatically shifts (most likely due to recognition and reversal). Some call it "the point of no return" for the central character (protagonist). Most often the protagonist makes a crucial moral decision that determines the outcome of the play. For example, when Oedipus demands to know the truth from the shepherd, he learns that he killed his father and married his mother. At this moment he undergoes *recognition* that he himself has caused the plague, which provides a *reversal of fortune* (*peripety*).

Climax: some artists use the term *climax* interchangeably with *crisis*, though a distinction may be made that the climax provides the highest point of emotion in the plot. The climax often coincides closely with the crisis point, and therefore the climax may be the inevitable confrontation between the protagonist and antagonist. For example, after Nora decides to let Torvald read the letter from Krogstad, he flies into a rage, providing a climactic confrontation between them. Nora discovers how Torvald truly sees her and how he sees their marriage (recognition), and she makes a decision to leave her home. Her status in the setting of her home has gone from high to low, a clear reversal of fortune.

Note that artists may have differing opinions of the climactic moment when they read the script, and only discover the true emotional climax upon staging the production. Some will argue that there is not a single climax, but a climax as well as a crisis in the beginning, middle, and end of the play, as Stanislavski does in his action analysis. Directors may also be advised to find the climax of each act or scene.

Falling Action (or *Dénouement*) and *Resolution*: the "fallout," or unraveling of action that follows the main crisis and ends the play. In *A Doll's House,* the falling action takes the form of a discussion between Nora and Torvald once she recognizes her true place in her home. She resolves the action of the play by leaving. Because the main conflict has already played out, the falling action and resolution often reveal the idea of the play, either through a lesson or a central question. Look to the end of the play and ask: Who wins? At what cost? Who is rewarded and who is punished? What does this tell us about the main dilemma in the play and how the outcome reflects the society of the time? What is the new status quo at the end of the play? Is balance or harmony restored?

Freytag, writing in the nineteenth century, differentiates between falling action and the final "catastrophe," which could also be considered the "resolution," separating it as the final action of the play. Examples could include Nora's door slam as she leaves her family, or Hedda Gabler's suicide – both striking events that punctuate the end of the play. While this writing technique was in vogue during the nineteenth century, not all plays have a clear resolution; in many contemporary plays, the falling action may purposefully leave us dangling rather than giving us a sense of closure. Such plays tend to raise questions rather than provide answers. Because plays end so differently, the graphic depiction of the ending may also differ, a consideration we will return to when we examine concept mapping in Part III.

Plot (Multi-linear): though it follows the structure of a causal plot, this term is sometimes used to distinguish plays that have two or more strong lines of action that run parallel to each other (Figure II.3). Usually both plot lines converge or intertwine by the play's end. An example of a multi-linear plot is Shakespeare's *Much Ado About Nothing,* in which the stories of two couples

Figure II.3   Multi-linear plot

(Hero/Claudio, Beatrice/Benedick) unfold in tandem. Though the couples proceed through different trials and tribulations in their relationships, the outcome of each story is similar: both couples love each other and wish to marry. As Shakespeare states in *A Midsummer Night's Dream*, "The course of true love never did run smooth" for either of the couples, an idea that connects the twin plots. Note that for centuries, playwrights (including Shakespeare) borrowed from other sources, combining more than one story into a new plot. It is unsurprising that such plays could in result in multi-linear plots.

Plot (Episodic): presents episodes, or scenes that are not related by cause-to-effect so much as by idea (Figure II.4). An episodic plot may reveal the story of one character through various episodes of his or her life, as is the case with *Abe Lincoln in Illinois* or the expressionistic play *Machinal*. Episodic plots may not come to any concrete conclusion, through they often finish with a sense of completeness, having played out a theme, much as a musical composition presents variations on a theme. Scenes may or may not be chronological and are often somewhat disconnected in terms of time span, location, central characters, or motif. For example, the Broadway musical *A Chorus Line* adheres to an episodic structure. In the musical, a group of dancers gather to audition for chorus parts in a Broadway musical. Rather than using cause-to-effect action to drive the plot forward, each character tell his or her own story of becoming a dancer, reflecting on the theme "What I Did for Love" (also the title of a song, which helps us achieve a sense of wholeness). The musical *Cats*

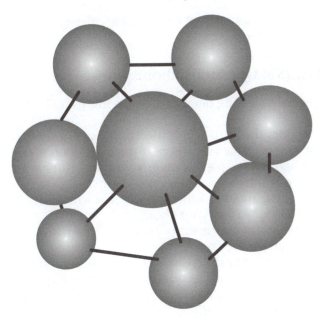

Figure II.4 Episodic plot

Note: This is an example of an episodic plot, with central dominate idea. Circles are purposefully different sizes, to reflect a variation in the episodes.

has a similar structure: each cat tells his or her story through song and dance.

Remember that the chronological order of scenes does not automatically signal a causal/linear plot; look to the connective tissue between scenes. Does one scene literally trigger the next, in a causal relationship? For example in *Machinal*, each scene depicts a young woman's journey through life, examining critical crossroads: her career, her life at home, her marriage, her motherhood, her affair, her trial, and her execution. The progression of scenes is chronological, but time is ill-defined, seemingly spanning several years. One scene does not necessarily trigger the next in a tight cause-to-effect link, rather the connective tissue that holds the plot together is the theme or idea: despair, brought on by the lack of choices that society gave a young woman of the period.

EXERCISE: Questions about plot

Answer the following questions, justifying your choices.

1. What does the initial exposition tell us about the given circumstances? How and where is the exposition revealed? Is it throughout the play, or mainly up front? Is there a state of balance or imbalance as the play begins?
2. What is the inciting action or incident which sets the plot into motion? Justify your choice.
3. What series of conflicts contribute to the rising action or complication?
4. What is the central crisis? Why is this central crisis the "point of no return?" Is human decision central to this crisis? If so, whose decision is it? Is there also recognition and reversal with the crisis?
5. Is the climax (highest emotional point) at the same point as the crisis, or a slightly different point? Are there other climactic moments, perhaps on a smaller scale?
6. What is the falling action? In other words, how does the action of the play change after the crisis?
7. How does the play conclude? Is there resolution, a major catastrophe and/or harmony restored? Does the play leave us with a sense of great loss (tragedy) or celebration (comedy)? Has the main character won or lost in pursuit of his/her goals? Are major questions left dangling or are solutions proposed? Is there a call to action or a moral?
8. Is your play causal/linear, multi-linear, episodic, or some variation? Use the relationships between scenes and overall structure of the plot to justify your answer. If it is an episodic play, the analysis above will not easily apply.

Character (as related to plot function)

Protagonist: the central character that drives the dramatic action forward. Though the term "tragic hero" is often equated with the protagonist, the hero is not without fault. Aristotle calls for the protagonist to be of high status and moral character, yet a fault of decision can cause the hero's downfall (see *hamartia* above). In modern drama, the protagonist need not be of high birth or high moral character, as is true of Nora in *A Doll's House*. Note that not all plays have a single or clear protagonist. For example, a group of characters may be seen as the protagonist, and in some cases artists may disagree on who the protagonist is and why. In *A Raisin in the Sun* playwright Lorraine Hansberry saw the protagonist as Mama, but actor Sidney Poitier argued that it was her son, Walter Lee, who drove the action of the play. Whose story is it? Quite often actors see their own characters as driving the action because they view the entire world of the play through the eyes of the character. Actors should be forewarned, therefore, to look to the structure of the entire play when identifying both protagonist and antagonist.

Antagonist: the character that struggles against or competes with the protagonist. This person need not be a "villain," but serves as an opposing force, causing the main conflict of the play. Note that it is the conflicting *ideas* of opposing forces that drive the dramatic action in a causal play. In literary study the central conflict may be described as man versus man (protagonist/antagonist), man versus nature, or man versus himself. In the latter case, the protagonist becomes his/her own antagonist.

Foil: a character (or characters) showing opposite traits to another main character, thereby providing contrast. For example, the two couples in *Much Ado About Nothing* are foils for one another. Whereas one couple (Hero and Claudio) is young, naïve, and sentimental, the other couple (Beatrice and Benedick) is older, more experienced, and more jaded.

Confidante: a character in whom another character confides. Often a friend, family member, or trusted servant, the confidante allows the audience to hear the true passions, problems, and secrets of a leading character. In *A Doll's House,* Kristine is Nora's confidante. It is because Nora confides in Kristine that we know her secret, her inner turmoil, and her point of view about herself and her husband.

Raisonneur: a character who serves as the mouthpiece for the playwright. Most often a raisonneur appears in didactic plays which drive home a lesson or point of view about a contentious issue. What is the author's perspective on the controversial matter? The raisonneur will provide it. Literally, the raisonneur is a person who reasons.

Normative (or *"Norm"*) *character:* in a play filled with otherwise odd or eccentric characters, this character gives a sense of what is "normal" for that culture or society. In essence, this character is also serving as a foil, showing the contrast of normal and abnormal behavior. In a comedy of manners, for example, the world is populated with idiots, charlatans, and the like, and often there is one character that is ordinary: the norm character. His or her name may help you identify the norm character, such as Alethea (Greek for truth) or Trueman (true-man).

EXERCISE: Questions about character function

1. Whose story is this? Is there a clear central figure (protagonist), or is it more of an ensemble piece? Explain.
2. Is there a clear antagonist? How does s/he oppose the protagonist and contribute to a conflict of ideas?
3. How do other characters in the play serve the following functions? (Not every type appears in every play.)
   - Foil
   - Confidante
   - Raisonneur
   - Norm character
4. Does the name of the character say something about him/her? If so, is this character also somewhat stereotyped? Explain.

Character (analysis)

In addition to understanding how the character functions in the plot, character analysis helps us determine the "character" of each character. Because the script is the only evidence used in formalist analysis, the artist must read the script multiple times, searching for clues and avoiding personal judgments. Search only for the facts in the script, which provide primary evidence. This approach also requires you to examine bias and change within the script. For example, does your character portray him/herself as honest, but behave deceptively? Do other characters see your character as duplicitous, or do they believe in his/her honesty? Does this perspective (from either side) change during the course of the play? Why? This analytical approach reveals hidden aspects of character that we may easily miss on a first or second reading of the play.

EXERCISE: Questions about character analysis

Choose one character and complete the following exercises.

Part A: Finding evidence

1. List any descriptive information from the playwright, such as appearance or demeanor (usually given upon the character's first entrance, if at all).
2. List everything a character says about him or herself.
3. List what other characters say about him/her.
4. List the character's actions and behaviors.

Part B: Key dimensions

Once you have listed all the evidence from the script, discuss character traits along four key dimensions:[4]

1. *Physical* – age, sex, build, race, hair color, health, etc.[5]
2. *Social* – class, status, relationships, job, education, religion/spirituality.
3. *Psychological*–desires/needs, conflict, willpower, self-concept, personality, qualities (sensitive, logical, gullible, etc.).
4. *Moral* – values and a sense where the character stands in terms of "right or wrong" behavior and "good or bad" ideas. These may overlap with a description of qualities such as honest, malicious, deceptive, self-righteous, and so on.

Part C: Visual component

Create a one-page collage for each main character. Be ready to explain how the collage identifies each character's four key dimensions.

Idea

Aristotle's third element in order of importance is often translated as *thought*, though *idea* and *theme* are also commonly used. Else translates from Aristotle: "This is the ability to state the issues and appropriate points pertaining to a given topic, an ability which springs from the arts of politics and rhetoric; in fact the earlier poets made their characters talk 'politically,' and the present-day poets rhetorically" (28). The idea of the play may argue a principal, teach us a lesson, or raise a central question. Though several themes and motifs may run through a play, one unifying idea usually underlies the entire work, sometimes referred to (in modern times) as the *spine*.

In addition to identifying the central idea and motifs of a play, pay attention to *how* idea is revealed. Is it primarily through language (see below), or are there symbols, sounds, images, and other metaphorical devices in the script? Is there a pattern in the way the ideas of the play are revealed? Does the title of the play allude to the main idea, as it does in *A Doll's House?* Also look for structural clues to the main idea. In Greek plays ideas initially arise in the dialogue between characters, but those ideas are explored or reflected upon in the choral odes.

Perhaps the goals of a character, as well as his/her victory or defeat in pursuing the goals, teaches us a lesson. Because the crisis provides a turning point in the plot and the resolution is the outcome of a central decision, these are good places to look for clues to ideas in causal plays. For example, we could argue that the crisis in *A Doll's House* is Nora's decision to let Torvald read the letter from Krogstad. There is no turning back, and the plot takes a drastic turn as a result. She has given in to revealing her deception, believing that her husband will save her in the end. Instead, he rails against her. Nora has a moment of recognition: Torvald does not view her as an equal or a helpmate, but as a deceiver who is poisoning their home and their children. The action reverses as Nora takes control of her own life, making the decision to leave her home and discover her own identity.

The idea may be condensed into a single word: for example, identity, sexism, or betrayal. More commonly, it is expressed as a phrase or sentence. For example, you could say that *A Doll's House* is a play about recognizing the difference between appearance and reality. Nora and Torvald's marriage and family may appear to be happy at the start of the play, but the reality proves to be different. The true mettle of each character is revealed through the moral and ethical challenges they face. At the crisis point, their façades are stripped away. Try to boil the play down to its essence: "This play is about _____."

It is important to recognize that not all plays state the idea overtly, and at times collaborators may disagree about the central idea. It is equally justifiable to say that *A Doll's House* is a play about women's lack of equality in society (though Ibsen wrote that his interest was not women's suffrage, but the rights of human beings). Issues of materialism, corruption, and deception are all ideas that surface within the play as well. In production, it is ultimately the director's interpretation of the central idea that determines its focus. A director who is true to the script forms his or her vision for the production by drawing from the ideas found within the script rather than trying to impose an idea upon it.

EXERCISE: Questions about idea

1. Does the play present an argument, teach us a lesson, or raise a central question? Consider the impression on the reader and potential audience.
2. How is the idea reflected in
   - the title
   - the characters
   - the crisis/resolution
   - the language
   - the symbolism?
3. Identify a sentence in the dialogue that relates the idea of the play.
4. What additional recurring motifs appear in the play?
5. Can you state the idea as a phrase or single word? Fill in the blank: It is a play about _____.
6. Nonverbal behaviors: think about the physical actions required in the play. How might the physicality of the actors (a stance, such as a character standing alone on stage, or

action sequence, such as a fight) also amplify the idea of the play? Remember that we are examining only what is called for in the script, not your own ideas about staging.

Language

Language is the verbal expression through which thought is conveyed. In drama it is primarily through dialogue or monologue, and occasionally through narration. In musicals or plays with music, it includes lyrics as well. Note that aural communication is considered as part of *music* and visual language, such as nonverbal expression, is considered as part of *spectacle* (both described below). Although there are overlapping concepts within Aristotle's elements, we will adhere to his original intent.

Language may be conveyed through verse or prose, and within these broad classifications, there are a number of variables to consider, including dialect, rhythm, rhyme, slang, and jargon. In addition, language can be concrete or abstract, formal or informal. Characters may speak in commands, questions, metaphors, or clichés. They may launch into long speeches or use short, staccato words to convey their thoughts. They may have asides to the audience or long monologues. They may state a main idea (or question) of the play, or speak in aphorisms.[6] All of these variables influence the way we describe the language of the play and the way we perceive individual characters; therefore theatre artists must pay careful attention to the language of the play. The language, of course, relates closely to the rhythm of the play, leading to the next element.

EXERCISE: Questions about language

Tip: Plays are written to be heard and not simply read, so as you answer Question 1, read sections of the play aloud to help you hear the play.

1. Describe the language of the play, synthesizing your thoughts. Use the following points to prepare your answer:
   • How does it vary from character to character? (For example, does one character speak in commands and another in metaphors and clichés?)

- Are there long monologues or asides?
- Is there narration?
- Is dialogue in verse (what kind?) prose, or both?
- Is there notable dialect, rhythm, rhyme, slang, or jargon?
- Is the language concrete or abstract? Formal or informal?
- Are sentences long, short, or fragmented?
- Does dialogue overlap?
- Are there pauses, or is silence used?

2. Prepare a scene or section to read aloud to a group, and be ready to give examples of how this scene supports your answer above.

Music (or aural elements)

Greek tragedy had a strong musical element, and Aristotle considered song composition "the greatest of the sensuous attractions" (Else 29). We now conceive of the music of the play to include not just literal music, but all aural (heard) elements in production. The rhythm of a dialect, the lyricism of a speech, the clashing of swords and the staccato barking of a dog are all examples of the aural elements of the play. Clearly, the work of the design team, director, and actors in production will greatly impact the aural elements that the audience perceives. In addition, the playwright's punctuation and stage directions also influence the way we hear the play in our heads when we read it from the page. The playwright's use of dashes, ellipses, or overlapping speech help us understand the rhythm of the play, and also affects our sense of tempo and mood. For example, David Mamet is known for his use of staccato speech. Listen to one of his movies, such as *Glengarry Glen Ross*. His characters can shift quickly to from speeches or monologues to dialogue filled with single words, phrases, or unfinished sentences. Through shifts in language and rhythm, Mamet peaks our curiosity about the nature of the characters' relationships.

As you read a play, look and listen for variation in sentence length, speech length, and vocal rhythm. Read the play aloud to help highlight these characteristics, listening acutely for patterns and changes. Imagine sound effects and music that are called for, considering how both the music of the language and the other aural elements combine to affect the overall tone or mood of the play.

EXERCISE: Questions about music

1. How does the language inform the overall musicality of the play? Consider how punctuation and silence also play into the dialogue. As in the previous exercise, read parts of the play aloud to find the aural elements.
2. What other aspects contribute to the aural elements of the production? List any sound effects and music mentioned in the script. *(Reminder: save artistic interpretation, such as desired underscoring, for design meetings; this is an analysis of the script itself.)*
3. a) How and why does the rhythm and tempo of the piece change through the play's progression? Explain how the aural elements of the play also affect the changing tone and mood. If a specific piece of music is called for, try to find an example of that piece to help you in your interpretation.

   b) Choose a scene or act of the play, read it aloud, and diagram your impression of the aural dynamics of each scene, paying close attention to the changing rhythm and tempo (for an example, see Figure II.5).[7] For example, a love scene may be slow and smooth, dictating a flowing line, whereas a fight scene may provoke you to draw a series of jagged lines. How is silence depicted in your diagram?

Figure II.5   Rhythm and tempo of a fight scene

Spectacle (or visual elements)

Along with music, spectacle is one of the least important elements Aristotle ascribed to his study of poetry, yet what we see and hear as an audience completely influences our perception of plot, character, idea, and language. Aristotle acknowledged that visual stimuli play a great role in the emotional effect of tragedy, but he had little regard for playwrights who relied on spectacle over a well-constructed plot. (In a similar manner today, critics often lament that fact that musicals and action movies bombard us with "eye candy" and visual stimuli rather than relying on a solid plot with well-drawn characters and intelligent dialogue.) Despite Aristotle's value judgments, we should consider the visual elements of the play as important elements of the script, even before it is produced. All elements of the visual – set, costumes, makeup, hair, lighting, props, special effects, and stage movement – are included in the conception of visual elements. What elements are called for in the script? How do they evoke atmosphere, tone, and mood, as well as a physical world for the play? Do they serve as central metaphors, as the seagull does in Chekhov's play of the same title?

Just because Aristotle attributed more value to plot and less to spectacle does not mean the same holds true of contemporary drama. In Part III we will see that modernist and postmodernist scripts often de-center the text, privileging what is seen and heard over the construct of plot. Other playwrights may favor character-driven plays, in which the relationships or journeys of the characters are central to driving the play. Still others stress idea over all else. Keep an open mind. Which element drives the play? What makes it work and holds our interest?

EXERCISE: Questions about spectacle

1. What visual spectacle is called for in the play? If there is large-scale spectacle, how is it used? To what end?
2. How do the visual elements evoke atmosphere, tone, and mood, as well as a physical world for the play?
3. Do any visual elements serve as central metaphors? Think of examples of plays or musicals that use this convention,

such as Mother Courage pulling her wagon in Brecht's play of the same name.
4. Present a collage that will help you explore the visual elements of the play. Include both abstract and concrete images, and incorporate at least one piece of art in your collage.

Stanislavski and the actor's script

Konstantin Stanislavski's so-called system became one of the primary sources of actor training in the United States by the mid-twentieth century. For decades, American academies and universities have been training student actors to "score" their scripts with Stanislavski's objectives, units, and beats. Many of us know his theories through Elizabeth Reynolds Hapgood's twentieth-century translations of his books. However, near the turn of the twenty-first century scholars gained access to newly opened Russian archives, and Stanislavski's major books were re-translated and freshly researched, most notably by Jean Benedetti and Sharon M. Carnicke. While these new publications allow us to see Stanislavski's work in a more authentic light, they also introduce some confusion about the jargon we have used and the assumptions we have made about Stanislavski's methods for the better part of the twentieth century.

Given the emphasis on Stanislavski in theatre training, theatre practitioners need to be familiar with his basic terminology, but in the newer Benedetti translation, some of the key terminology has changed. When someone talks about *beats* and *units*, we need to understand that they were originally described as *small bits* and *large bits*. Reportedly, when Russian teachers brought Stanislavski's methods to Americans, their accents caused the term *bit* to be heard and notated as *beat*. Furthermore, Hapgood made adjustments of her own, translating larger divisions of the text as *units*, though Benedetti remains true to Stanislavski and retains the word *bits* (Benedetti xviii).[8]

In *An Actor Prepares,* Stanislavski presents his theories through the narrative voice of a young acting student going to class with his director/teacher, Torstov. In Chapter 5 Torstov uses the metaphor of a cooked turkey being torn apart into bits at the dinner table to emphasize that the play has distinctive parts. In this metaphorical story, several gluttonous youths cram down large pieces of turkey all at once, choking. They are warned to "cut it up into smaller and smaller [pieces]" and if the meat is dry, to "spice it up with the beauty of your imagination, your own ideas" (Benedetti 136). After hearing this story, the acting student heads home, thinking about what he learned. He tries to divide each of his actions into bits: going down stairs, walking down the street, opening the door to his apartment, and so on. He quickly realizes that there are too many bits; the number of small actions is overwhelming. The next day, the student goes back to his director for clarification about how to divide the bits of a play. Torstov advises, "The actor... must not go by the small Bits which are numerous and which cannot all be remembered, but by the large, most important Bits, through which the creative path passes" (139). In the narrator's example, "going home" is the larger bit (which Hapgood translated as *unit*), made up of smaller bits (which she called *beats*).

Torstov warns his students that the smaller bits are a preparatory measure of the actor, and that the bits must be put back together into a cohesive whole or the actor will become lost in a sea of detail. "[G]o from one large Bit to the next without losing sight of the final goal," he advises (142). In other words, the bits (*beats*) follow a logical progression, as do the larger bits (*units*), to form a cohesive whole. Furthermore, Torstov asks his students to name the bits, advising that they find the essential quality for each bit and distill it.

Because *beats* and *units* have now become standard terms in acting, we will revert to that terminology from here on. Note that a beat in music has a different meaning, as does taking a beat (a pause) when reading a scene; these should not be confused with Stanislavski's definition.

For beginners, the most difficult part of identifying beats and units is not understanding the concept, but applying it, for there are no hard and fast rules about the size of each section. Traditional plays are usually divided into acts and scenes. Each scene can be further divided into French scenes each time a character enters or exits. Scenes and French scenes can further be divided into major sections (units) and each unit into beats. A beat change usually occurs if/when:

- the topic changes
- the action or tactic of a character changes
- the character has physical "business" on stage without dialog, such as Nora dancing the tarentella in *A Doll's House*
- another character enters or leaves (though this may signal a larger, unit change)

Using Michael Meyer's translation of *A Doll's House* as an example, consider the following dialog from Act I, Scene 1, between Nora and her husband, Torvald Helmer. As the play opens, Nora arrives with her parcels and tips the porter generously, which could be considered as the first beat of the scene. The second beat begins as she flirts with Torvald through his closed office door, trying to get his attention. She begins by humming a tune.

HELMER   *(from his room)*: Is that my little skylark twittering out there?

NORA   *(opening some of the parcels)*: It is!

HELMER: Is that my squirrel rustling?

NORA: Yes!

HELMER: When did my squirrel come home?

NORA: Just now. *(Pops the bag of macaroons into her pocket and wipes her mouth.)* Come out here, Torvald, and see what I've bought.

HELMER: You musn't disturb me! *(Short pause, then he opens the door and looks in, his pen in his hand.)* Bought, did you say? All that? Has my little squanderbird been overspending again?

NORA: Oh. Torvald, surely we can let ourselves to a little this year! It's the first Christmas we don't have to scrape.

HELMER: Well, you know, we can't afford to be extravagant.

NORA: Oh yes, Torvald, we can be a little extravagant now. Can't we? Just a tiny bit? You've got a big salary now, and you're going to make lots and lots of money.

HELMER: Next year, yes. But my new salary doesn't start till April.

NORA: Pooh! We can borrow till then.

We might call this first unit "Nora and her spending." Smaller beats might be labeled:

1) Nora arrives with parcels;
2) Torvald flirts with Nora; and
3) Nora argues for extravagance.

Nora and Torvald's argument continues in this unit of "Nora and her spending," with Nora changing tactics as she tries to justify her need for more money. Depending on how detailed the analysis is, each tactic (refuting, pouting, begging, etc.) could be considered a beat change. Note that active and playable verbs are used to describe beats, because they describe what characters are actually *doing*.

In addition to breaking down beats and units, it is important to recognize Stanislavski's emphasis on studying the *given circumstances*, or facts about the world of the play. Just as a journalist determines the "who, what, when, and where" for a story, the theatre artist should identify the facts that make up the imaginary world of the play. Usually, the bulk of this information is gathered in the exposition, both at the beginning of the play and sprinkled throughout, depending on the playwright's writing technique. For example, Ibsen provides important information in the opening dialogue of *A Doll's House*, but he also writes lengthy stage directions that describe the play's setting. The description before Act I helps set the mood for the scene as well as establishing information about the Helmers' house:

> *A comfortably and tastefully, but not expensively furnished room. Backstage right a door leads out to the hall: backstage left, another door to* HELMER'S *study. Between these two doors stands a piano. In the middle of the left-hand wall, slightly upstage, is a door; downstage of this, against the same wall, a stove lined with porcelain tiles, with a couple of armchairs and a rocking-chair in front of it. Between the stove and the side door is a small table. Engravings on the wall. A what-not with china and other bric-a-brac; a small bookcase with leather-bound books. A carpet on the floor; a fire in the stove. A winter day.*

> *A bell rings in the hall outside. After a moment, we hear the front door being opened.* NORA *enters the room, humming contentedly to herself. She is wearing outdoor clothes and carrying a lot of parcels, which she puts down on the table right. She leaves the door to the hall open; through it, we can see a* PORTER *carrying a Christmas tree and a basket. He gives these to the* MAID, *who has opened the door for them.*

We now know the season, the specific holiday, the relative temperatures inside and out, something of the socioeconomic status of the owners, their taste in décor, and the mood of Nora as she enters. We can begin to imagine ourselves in this time and place based on the facts given to us.

Realistic playwrights are known for adding a vast amount of detail to their plays through stage directions. However, there is a warning about stage directions: for a significant part of the twentieth century, publishers (rather than playwrights) added stage directions, describing the artists' interpretations from an original production.[9] Often these refer to physical staging or the emotional interpretation of a line, for example, *"sitting"* or *"storming off."* When studying a script for production, artists are often instructed to cross out or disregard stage directions because it is difficult to know their true source, and it can restrict their interpretation. One option is to ignore the staging and emotional descriptions, while paying attention to the descriptions of setting and character, as these are likely the playwright's additions. In the case of a play with several translations or adaptations, such as *A Doll's House*, it is worthwhile to compare versions.

EXERCISE: Units, beats, and given circumstances

1. Form a group and choose one scene to divide into units and beats, giving titles to each. Work on the divisions and titles individually or in pairs, then regroup and compare notes. Did your divisions match? Be prepared to justify your divisions and titles. How do the units and beats contribute to the action of the play as a whole? (For example, how is

> the character's action contributing to an overarching goal?)
> Have you used active, playable verbs in your beat titles?
> 2. What are the given circumstances (the who, what, when,
>   where) of the play, and how are they revealed? Do the char-
>   acters give their own ideas about the world of the play? Are
>   those ideas biased, and does the bias change by the play's
>   end?

Action analysis

In the third edition of his script analysis book Thomas included –
for the first time in English – a description of Stanislavski's action
analysis, which Stanislavski's former student, Maria Knebel,
completed after his death. Disenchanted with the extensive
table work that the Moscow Art Theatre had adopted based on
his early methods, Stanislavski sought a more succinct approach
to the text, primarily through plot and idea. He determined that
"mental investigation" was only part of the discovery of the
play, which was made whole through a "physical investigation"
in rehearsal, producing a "psychophysical unity" of the creative
process (Thomas xxviii).[10] Further study of Thomas' book is recommended before conducting an action analysis; quotations are
from the definitions that correspond to Thomas' fourth edition.

Action analysis takes the reader through a course of both concrete and abstract investigation. The major steps may be sum-
marized as:

- listing the sequence of external events
- reviewing the facts (given circumstances, background story)
- identifying the seed of the play
- listing the sequence of internal events, linked to the seed
- identifying three major climaxes
- deriving the theme and super-objective of the play
- stating the through-action and counter through-action

My own students have found that action analysis can be tricky,
particularly in finding a seed that links to all the internal events,
but the rewards from the analysis are enlightening and worthwhile. Consider working with a partner or a small group the

first time you try action analysis. Conduct your own analysis first, then get together and compare notes. Whose seed fits the best and why? Which of the three major climaxes fits best and why? Work together to wordsmith the super-objective, through-action, and counter through-action. Discussing such issues not only helps you articulate your viewpoint, but helps you work on collaborative interpretation of the play, which is crucial to theatre practice.

Brief definitions of each step are given below, with my own examples drawn from Mel Brooks' and Tom Meehan's Tony Award-winning musical, *The Producers*.[11] For those who are unfamiliar with the musical, the basic plot is fairly simple. Max Bialystock, a boisterous down-and-out Broadway producer, convinces Leo Bloom, a mousy accountant, to join him in an underhanded scheme: to raise extra money for a Broadway flop, close the show, and skip town. When their flop becomes an unexpected hit, Max lands in jail and Leo flees, but returns and confesses at the trial. In prison, they follow their passion and produce a musical, returning to produce on Broadway after their jail sentence (and thereby providing the traditional happy ending of an old-fashioned musical comedy).

> *Sequence of external events*: the major physical/material events that move the plot forward. This is a list of "short and snappy" phrases showing the progression of the action, such as "arrivals or departures, meetings, announcements, discussions, quarrels, etc." (Thomas 4). For example, external events for *The Producers*, Act I are:
>
> 1.1 Max vows to regain power.
> 1.2 Max begs Leo to join him in a swindling scheme.
> 1.3 Leo fanatisizes about being a Broadway producer.
> 1.4 Max and Leo celebrate a new-found partnership.
> 1.5 Max and Leo find a sure-fire flop: *Springtime for Hitler*.
> 1.6 Franz (the author) signs a Broadway contract.
> 1.7 Roger is manipulated into directing *Springtime for Hitler*.
> 1.8 Ulla auditions and becomes a temporary secretary.
> 1.9 Max raises money by seducing little old ladies as backers.

Reviewing the facts: considering the "who, what, when, where, why, and how" of the play. This includes given circumstances and background story, so it is not only what happens in the play, but an examination of the world of the play and events that occur outside of the plot (Thomas 6).

Seed: the kernel, or essence of the play, distilled down to a single word. As the main idea, the seed must link to the dramatic action of every episode. Vladimir Nemirovich-Danchenko, cofounder of the Moscow Art Theatre, argued that the creative work of the production team must stem from the director's pronouncement of the seed, providing a "harmonic unity of all its parts" (Knebel quoted in Thomas, 8). Although there may be different interpretations of *The Producers,* I have identified the seed as "obsession."

Sequence of internal events: how the seed is operating beneath the surface of external events. Thomas writes, "Indeed, an *internal event* is defined as the expression of the seed growing within the external event" (12). Note that if the seed you have chosen does not connect to each major event, you have not found a true seed that permeates the action of the play, and must go back to find the true seed. In the example below from *The Producers*, the external event is stated first, and underneath the internal event is in italics, with the seed underlined.

1.1 Max vows to regain power.

Max reveals his <u>obsession</u> with making a comeback.

1.2 Max begs Leo to join him in a swindling scheme.

Max's <u>obsession</u> with money drives him to crime.

1.3 Leo fanatisizes about being a Broadway producer.

Leo's subconscious <u>obsession</u> with a glamorous life surfaces.

1.4 Max and Leo celebrate a new-found partnership.

Max and Leo celebrate their shared <u>obsession</u> about pulling off the scheme.

1.5 Max and Leo find a sure-fire flop: Springtime for Hitler.

Max and Leo <u>obsess</u> over choosing the right script.

1.6 Franz (the author) signs a Broadway contract.

Franz reveals his <u>obsession</u> with restoring Hitler's name.

1.7 Roger is manipulated into directing *Springtime for Hitler.*

Roger reveals his <u>obsession </u>with recognition and prestige.

1.8 Ulla auditions and becomes a temporary secretary.

Max and Leo <u>obsess</u> over the voluptuous Ulla.

1.9 Max raises money by seducing little old ladies as backers.

Max's <u>obsession</u> with money matches the backers' <u>obsession</u> with sex.

Three major climaxes: identifying climaxes in the beginning, middle, and end of the play, pushing the action of the play forward. Thomas explains, "The first stage dramatizes the overall goal of the main character, the second stage shows the hardships encountered by the main character in pursuit of this goal, and the third stage enacts how the main character comes to terms with the play's particular reality" (15). Identifying the climaxes at the beginning and end first may help you identify the climax between the two. In *The Producers*, the following acts/scenes provide the plot's major climaxes. (Predictably, each climactic moment also coincides with a song, for in musical theatre, when emotions escalate to the point that they can no longer be contained, a song and/or dance springs forth.)

1.3 Leo joins in the obsession and commits to the scheme.
     (Song: *I Wanna Be A Producer.*)

2.5 The "hit" status of their show wreaks havoc with the scheme.
     (Song: *Where Did We Go Right?*)

2.7 Leo turns himself in, supporting Max, but leading to their joint imprisonment.
     (Song: *'Til Him.*)

Theme: "the play's response to the seed, what the play shows about the seed.... The three major climaxes provide the best path to understanding the theme of the play" (Thomas 20).

If the seed is *obsession,* the theme is *blind obsession.* In *The Producers,* the morally upright Leo resists Max's underhanded scheme, but his obsession with the glamorous life of a producer (gloriously revealed in a fantasy sequence[)] blinds him, and he abandons his morals (climax one). Max's and Leo's obsession with their scheme blinds them to their inevitable downfall – the turning point in the plot (climax two) – and to their guilty verdict (climax three). Musicals typically appeal strongly to emotions, so it is notable that Brooks and Meehan insert an emotional ballad from Max, *Betrayed,* before climax three, just before Leo turns himself in, singing his own touching ballad of support and friendship, *'Til Him.*

Super-objective: the protagonist's overarching goal. The theme of the play is enveloped in the protagonist's pursuit of the goal, therefore the statement of super-objective gives a sense of forward motion (the pursuit). Having hit rock bottom, Max's (and ultimately Leo's) super-objective becomes *to cheat the system and win at all costs.* In this particular case, Max must have Leo's support to make the scheme work; one could say the two-person team of *The Producers* is the protagonist in this sense, and perhaps the title to the piece is a clue to that end. Though they are foils for each other, this team works as a unit to achieve a joint goal. Note that the super-objective also relates to the theme, blind obsession, though theme need not be overtly stated in the super-objective.

Through-action (or *through-line*): "A one sentence description of the main conflict, expressing what the main character does in the play to accomplish his/her super-objective" (Thomas 23). The through-action marries the facts of the play to the central action, describing what happens. A possible statement of through-action in *The Producers* is: "Overcome by the desire for a better life, Max and Leo pursue an underhanded scheme to cheat their backers with a Broadway flop."

Counter through-action: describes the opposing force to the through-action – the action running against the protagonist, providing the conflict. Ask yourself who provides the obstacle(s) to the main character's goal. The opposing force may be a single character as the antagonist, or may not, as is the case in *The Producers:* "Obsessed with producing the worst show on Broadway, Max and Leo go too far, creating a satirical hit and undermining their own corrupt scheme."

In practice, action analysis is effective and efficient, or as Thomas writes, "a speedy way of getting to the professional guts of a play" (23), though it is not detailed enough in all areas (such as language) to serve as the only means of analysis. With its attention to seed, theme, and multiple climaxes, action analysis can provide interesting insights into nonlinear plays as well, particularly when partnered with physical exploration of the play, as Stanislavski intended.[12] That being said, action analysis presupposes that there is a central character pursuing a single goal with a through-line of action, which is not always the case in nonlinear plays, as we shall see in Part III.

EXERCISE: Action analysis paper

Write a five page action analysis for a play you are exploring. You will need to summarize your findings, but also back up your claims with specific examples from the script. Remember to cite all material for any quoted or paraphrased passages and include a list of works cited. Budget your time in advance in order to 1) think through the assignment; 2) analyze the play; 3) write the draft; and 4) refine the draft.

Use the action analysis section of this book to organize your paper. You are not to conduct outside research, but to work primarily from the script and this book or any other assigned reading (such as Thomas). Put any lists, such as a list of external and internal events, in an appendix, summarizing your findings in the paper itself.

Questions for application

- How does the play you are studying compare with Aristotle's definition in terms of seriousness? Do the main characters' actions lead to catharsis?

- Does your play have a distinct beginning, middle, and end? If so, explain where you divide these larger parts of the plot and why at these junctions.
- Does the plot include reversal and recognition? If so, justify at what points in the plot. Identify what *type* of discovery is made and whether the plot is simple or complex based on Aristotle's definition.
- Is there a tragic hero of high character and reputation? What is his error in judgment (*hamartia*)? Does the character fit his/her reality (showing appropriate decorum), and remain consistent?
- Is the play a classical tragedy, a modern tragedy, a comedy, or some other genre?
- What does the initial exposition tell us about the given circumstances? How and where is the exposition revealed? Is it throughout the play, or mainly up front? Is there a state of balance or imbalance as the play begins?
- What is the inciting action or incident, which sets the plot into motion?
- What series of conflicts contribute to the rising action, or complication?
- What is the central crisis? Why is this central crisis the "point of no return?" Is human decision central to this crisis? If so, whose decision is it? Is there also recognition and reversal with the crisis?
- Is the climax (highest emotional point) at the same point as the crisis, or slightly different point? Are there other climactic moments, perhaps on a smaller scale?
- What is the falling action? In other words, how does the action of the play change after the central crisis?
- How does the play conclude? Is there resolution, a major catastrophe and/or harmony restored? Has the main character won or lost in pursuit of his/her goals? Are major questions left dangling or are solutions proposed? Is there a call to action or a moral?
- Is your play causal/linear, multi-linear, episodic, or does it have a unique structure, such as circular?[13]

- Whose story is this? Is there a clear central figure (protagonist), or is it more of an ensemble piece?
- Is there a clear antagonist? How does s/he oppose the protagonist and provide a conflicting idea in the play?
- How do other characters in the play serve the following functions: foil, confidante, raisonneur, norm character. (Not every type appears in every play.)
- Does the name of the character say something about him/her? If so, is this character also portrayed as a stereotype?
- What kind of evidence about character comes from the script, and how is it biased?
  1. Descriptive information from playwright (usually physical)
  2. What the character says about him or herself
  3. What other characters say about him/her
  4. The character's actions and behaviors
- What are the physical, social, psychological, and moral dimensions of the character(s)?
- How does the language inform the overall musicality of the play? Consider how punctuation and silence also play into the dialogue.
- What other aspects contribute to the aural elements of the production?
- How and why does the rhythm or tempo of the piece change through the play's progression? How do the aural elements of the play also affect the changing tone and mood?
- What visual spectacle is called for in the play? If there is large-scale spectacle, how is it used?
- How do the visual elements evoke an atmosphere, tone, and mood, as well as a physical world for the play?
- Do any visual elements serve as central metaphors?
- Does one element (plot, character, idea, language, music, spectacle) drive the play? What makes it work and holds our interest?
- What are the given circumstances (the "who, what, when, where") of the play, and how are they revealed? Do the characters give their own ideas about the world of the play? Are they biased, and does the bias change by the play's end?

- What are the units, or large bits of the play? How can you label them as they relate to the action of the play?
- What are the smaller bits, or beats? How can you label them as they relate to the action of the play? How do the units and beats add up to the whole of the play?
- How can Stanislavski's action analysis help you understand the play? Identify:
  - o Sequence of external events
  - o Facts from the play
  - o Seed
  - o Sequence of internal events
  - o Three major climaxes
  - o Theme
  - o Super-objective
  - o Through-action
  - o Counter through-action.

Notes

1. See Thomas' introduction for more information about the etymology of the word and for distinctions between *formal, formalist,* and *formalistic.* His book provides numerous definitions, examples, and questions related to formalist analysis.
2. An interesting use of Aristotle can be found in the user-friendly book, *Aristotle's Poetics for Screenwriters,* by Michael Tierno. Though it addresses film rather than theatre, the same principles apply.
3. Note that while tragedy and comedy were the two primary genres in Aristotle's time, others have developed over the centuries, such as melodrama, farce, and tragicomedy. In the eighteenth century, Denis Diderot used the term *drame bourgoise* (commonly known now simply as *drama*) to describe an emerging genre that dealt with the moral issues of middle-class characters. Though most modern writers do not concern themselves with purity of genre, historical playwrights often did.
4. Oscar Brockett originally outlined these four major characteristics in his book *The Theatre: An Introduction,* and he in turn adapts his classifications from author Hubert Heffner (*Modern Theatre Practice*) and others.

5. Francis Hodge includes "character-mood-intensity," describing the physical state of the body: nervous stomach, light shallow breathing, etc. Though these states may be alluded to in the text, some may be conjecture on the part of the performer. For further information, see Hodge and McLain's *Play Directing: Analysis, Communication, and Style*.

6. Mirriam-Webster's online dictionary defines *aphorism* as "1. a concise statement of a principle; 2. a terse formulation of a truth or sentiment: adage." For example, "All's well that ends well," or "Better to be safe than sorry."

7. This exercise is a variation of one used by Francis Hodge for recording tempos. See Hodge and McLain's *Play Directing: Analysis, Communication, and Style* for further exploration of tempo, rhythm, and mood.

8. Benedetti also chronicles the issue of Soviet censorship of Stanislavski's work, as does Carnicke. The result was that much of his influence from yoga and spirituality was cut from his early publications.

9. Professor Kristine Holtvedt, Purdue University, reports that according to Harold Scott, the practice of adding stage directions from productions ended in 1980. Scott is the former Head of the Directing Program at Mason Gross School of the Arts, Rutgers, The State University of New Jersey.

10. Phillip B. Zarrilli adds that in modern Russia, teachers following the methods of Stanislavski emphasize his later work with physical action rather than placing too much emphasis on intellectual analysis (Zarrilli 12).

11. In order to provide as many types of examples as possible, I thought it fitting – and somewhat refreshing – to include a musical comedy. For the complete libretto and an account of how *The Producers* transitioned from film to Broadway, see Brooks and Meehan (2001).

12. Thomas states, "action analysis is the intellectual part of Stanislavski's Active Analysis" (xxvi). For more information on Active Analysis, see Sharon M. Carnicke's *Stanislavski in Focus*.

13. Absurdist playwrights often create a circular plot structure, reflecting the fact that in life we toil in vain. Consider Samuel Beckett's *Waiting for Godot*: the play begins and ends with two characters waiting for Godot, who never arrives. (Part III gives further consideration to nontraditional structures.)

Sources and further study

Ball, David. *Backwards and Forwards: A Technical Manual for Reading Plays.* Carbondale, IL: Southern Illinois University Press, 1983.

Benedetti, Jean, ed. and trans. *An Actor's Work.* By Konstantin Stanislavski. London: Routledge, 2008.

Brockett, Oscar. *The Theatre: An Introduction.* 3rd ed. New York: Holt, Rinehart and Winston, 1979.

Brooks, Mel and Thomas Meehan. *The Producers: The Book, Lyrics and Story Behind the Biggest Hit in Broadway History.* New York: Hyperion, 2001.

Carnicke, Sharon M. *Stanislavski in Focus.* 1st ed. Amsterdam: Hardwood Academic, 1998; 2nd ed. published by London: Routledge, 2008.

Cooper, Lane. *The Poetics of Aristotle: Its Meaning and Influence.* Westport, CT: Greenwood, 1923.

Else, Gerald F., trans. *Aristotle: Poetics.* By Aristotle. Ann Arbor, MI: University of Michigan Press, 1967.

——. *Aristotle's Poetics: The Argument.* Cambridge: Harvard University Press, 1957.

Freytag, Gustav. *Freytag's Technique of the Drama.* Trans. Elias J. MacEwan. New York: Benjamin Blom [1863] 1968.

Halliwell, Stephen, trans. *The Poetics of Aristotle: Translation and Commentary.* Chapel Hill, NC: University of North Carolina Press, 1987.

Hodge, Francis and Michael McLain. *Play Directing: Analysis, Communication, and Style.* 7th ed. Boston, MA: Allyn and Bacon, 2009.

Ibsen, Henrik. *A Doll's House.* Trans. Michael Meyer. In *Ghosts, and Three Other Plays.* Garden City, NY: 1966.

Levin, Irina and Levin, Igor. *The Stanislavski Secret.* Colorado Springs: Merriwether, 2002.

McLeish, Kenneth. *Poetics.* By Aristotle. New York: TCG, 1998, 1999.

Sergel, Christopher. *To Kill A Mockingbird.* Based on a novel by Harper Lee. Portsmouth, NH: Heinemann, 1995.

Thomas, James. *Script Analysis for Actors, Directors and Designers.* 3rd and 4th edns. Burlington, MA: Focal/Elsevier, 2005, 2009.

Tierno, Michael. *Aristotle's Poetics for Screenwriters.* New York: Hyperion, 2002.

Zarilli, Phillip B., ed. *Acting (Re)considered: A Theoretical and Practical Guide.* 2nd ed. London: Routledge, 2002.

III

Interpreting the Nonlinear Play

This section of the book addresses strategies for the interpretation of nonlinear plays, which have proliferated in modern and postmodern eras. Our study begins with terminology, then moves to postmodernism before examining various facets of the plays to consider: form and content, visualization of the structure, vocality, and various methods for addressing interpretation. Be forewarned that there is no single formula or method for interpreting nonlinear plays, for the forms and styles vary widely; usually our interpretive and visceral responses are more important than traditional forms of textual analysis, particularly when working with postmodern plays. We can form a better grasp of how these plays work through examining the work of playwrights and directors who work with nonlinear scripts. Finding the right questions to ask and conducting exercises with the text will add to our tools of discovery.

Nonlinear by any other name

I have used the term *nonlinear* because it is fairly common, referring to a play that does not rely on a cause-to-effect relationship to create a tight through-line of action in the plot. Note, however, that a play may be nonlinear in structure but still present the scenes in rough chronological order; it is the causal link between scenes that is missing. For example, in Maria Irene Fornes' play *Fefu and Her Friends,* a group of women gather at Fefu's house to plan an event. A series of scenes unfolds about the relationships among the women and about their own identities. The scenes could be considered in loose chronological order when reading the play, but each scene does not hinge on its predecessor in order to tell the story; rather, the plot is episodic in nature.

The issue of terminology is not an easy one, and it plagues both novices and professionals. A nonlinear play may also be called *noncausal, episodic, nonrealistic* (reacting against Realism), or *postdramatic,* though connotations vary.[1] In his book *New Playwriting Strategies: A Language-Based Approach to Playwriting* (2001), Paul C. Castagno uses *language playwrights* and *new playwrights* to describe nontraditional writing, citing such figures as Mac Wellman, Len Jenkin, Eric Overmyer, Suzan-Lori Parks, and Paula Vogel. He notes that while their writing has been highly influential in theatrical circles, their success in mainstream theatre (for the most part) has been limited. Plays that deviate from a linear/causal structure might also be described as *hybrids,* combining more than one structure. For example, a hybrid play could begin with a realistic/causal plot, then deviate to abstract episodes with little internal connection and a nebulous, non-conclusive ending. To make matters more complex, a nonlinear play may be further categorized as modern, postmodern, or even post-postmodern, depending on its period and distinguishing characteristics. Whatever the nomenclature, nonlinear plays must be understood on their own terms. Much like fingerprints, no two plays are alike; it is our job as theatre practitioners to decipher and interpret their unique aspects.

Because of each play's unique character, we will examine several playwrights and their writing techniques, as well as several directors' methods of interpretation for production. First, we turn our attention to postmodernism, which has had a significant impact on contemporary playwriting.

Postmodernism

Although many people are familiar with the term *postmodern* (*po-mo*) because it is so often used in our society, trying to explain postmodernism is difficult at best, for there is no concrete definition. Quite literally, the term connotes moving beyond the modernist movement of the late nineteenth to mid-twentieth century. Because modernism was characterized as a break from traditional forms, the meaning of postmodernism seems even more esoteric. What does it mean to move beyond the modernist reaction to traditional forms?

In theatre, as in other arts, we can study specific modernist movements, such as symbolism, futurism, dadaism, surrealism, and expressionism; they are defined movements with specific theoretical underpinnings (sometimes including manifestos) and specific characteristics. Part of the concept of postmodernism is moving beyond one single conception of art – what theatre can or should be – to a pluralistic conception. A postmodern performance could combine elements from past modernist movements and also layer on new perspectives. To clarify this issue, let's compare a modernist and postmodernist conception of sound design. The Italian Futurists were part of the modernist movement of the early twentieth century, and Luigi Russolo's Futurist manifesto of 1913 made specific demands about how music should be construed in performance. Russolo embraced the war effort, industry, and the modern city, and dictated that the Art of Noise – machines, jackhammers, guns, airplane motors, and the like – be embraced as music in a Futurist performance. In contrast, a postmodernist might use machine noise as well, but juxtapose it with jingles from television commercials, jarring us from the realm of industry to the realm of trite popular culture and media. With postmodernism, no longer is there a single notion of what art can or should be. Postmodern artists enjoy an unbridled freedom of expression, often layering associations that do not have logical connections.

A related premise in postmodern thought is that there is no single "truth," just as there is no single way to approach the creation of an artistic work. Meaning is made through the perception of the spectator/audience and does not reside with the artist/creator. Symbols and their interpretations take on more importance than the plot, which Aristotle considered the most important element. The text is no longer the leading path to follow; in fact, it may be an element to play against, effectively *de-centering* the text from its former primary position. In other words, what you see, hear, smell, touch and sense in a postmodern production likely bears much more meaning than the plot or action of the play. Reading a postmodern script, therefore, relies not upon following the proverbial trail of breadcrumbs from beginning to end, but on our more abstract ability to interpret and synthesize our impressions as we see/hear/sense the production in our mind's eye. The metaphorical "breadcrumbs" are now taking shape at will, blown away from their original trail, into new patterns with many possibilities.

One of the clearest introductory books on postmodernism for theatre practitioners is Jon Whitmore's *Directing Postmodern Theater* (1994), in part because he gives examples of the characteristics of postmodern performance. Whitmore explains, "For postmodernists, extended modernist principles include widespread experimentation of collage, atonality, nonlinearity, decenteredness, imbalance, skepticism, abstractness, ambiguity, serialization, stream-of-consciousness, and the like. Postmodernist principles that reject modernism include the highlighting of self-referentiality, deconstruction, and popular culture (rejecting the notion that high art is the only art worth investigating)" (Whitmore 3). To add to the description, in *Beginning Theory* (1995) Peter Barry explains that postmodernism often has a tone of celebrating fragmentation, whereas modernist fragmentation, born during the eras of World War I and II, is often bleak in tone. Barry also references Jean Baudrillard's theory of "the loss of the real," which impacts postmodern thought. In a world in which we airbrush supermodels on magazine covers, this sense of something being "real" yet simultaneously "fabricated" is clear.[2]

Taking another approach, sociologist Laurel Richardson uses the metaphor of crystallization to exemplify the search for "truth" in a postmodern world:

> Crystals are prisms that reflect externalities and refract within themselves, creating different colors, patterns, arrays, casting off in different directions. What we see depends upon our angle of repose.... Crystallisation, without losing structure,

de-constructs the traditional idea of validity (we feel how there is no single truth, we see how texts validate themselves); and crystallisation provides us with a deepened, complex, thoroughly partial, understanding of the topic. Paradoxically, we know more and doubt what we know. (522)

An example of a postmodern text that exhibits Richardson's concept of crystallization and Baudrillard's "loss of the real" is Martin Crimp's play, *Attempts on Her Life* (1997). Crimp started by writing short, individual scenes about a person named Anne (alternately called Annie, Anna, or Anya). He then gathered the work together, forming 17 open scenarios with lines on the page, but no assigned characters or settings. Anne's identity constantly changes as she is referenced in each scene, yet she never clearly presents her own voice. She is alternately characterized as a caring mother, an adventurous daughter, a seductress, a celebrity, an automaton, an avant-garde artist, a terrorist, and even a car. In other words, there is no single character, Anne. She seems to be a construct of crystallized facets, and the performers and audience are left to their own devices when deciphering the play. What does it all mean? There is no one meaning; it resides in each of us. Adding to the sense of postmodernity, the dialogue alludes to media culture – cameras panning, or going in for close-ups – making us wonder if the performance is a construction of a media event. Much like the airbrushed model in the previous example, we are aware that a "spin" or meta-theatrical devise may be at work. Anne/Anya/Annie is being variously constructed and simultaneously deconstructed. The minute we think we understand who she is, another scene tears down that construction. We are left at odds with what to believe. To make matters more baffling, the last scenario in the play presents no closure. Crimp presents two simultaneous sets of lines on the last page of the text: one about a man who brings his child to "watch him murder this other child's mother" and one about the meaning of "fresh" versus "previously frozen" salmon (Crimp 86). The mind boggles as it tries to put the pieces together, because the pieces do not fit neatly, nor are they meant to fit.

Postmodern scripts can frustrate both audiences and theatre artists as we try to understand and interpret what is not literal and linear. Our brains want to make order out of disorder, seeking to create meaning. Directors Anne Bogart and Tina Landau explain that categorizing the world helps us feel in control, and yet attaching labels (comedy, tragedy, linear, episodic, protagonist, antagonist – and many more) can also make us blind to shades of differentiation. Writers do not necessarily sit down and think, "I'm going to write a linear, realistic play with a clear protagonist and antagonist." Indeed, artists of all sorts are inspired to write from a variety of instincts. English professor Mary Rose O'Reilley explains:

> Personal writing leads us to see multiple levels in the house of truth: we deal in versions of reality. We settle on a story we can live with, not only because it's hard to be honest but also because our minds keep trying to create order. Order, as any freshman writer knows requires us to craft a beginning, middle, and end, with transitional devices in place to ensure coherence. Organization, then, always violates, to some degree, the Real. (10)

EXERCISE: The loss of the real

1. "Reality television" is a clear case of the media presenting us with something that purports to be real, but is not. With a partner or small group, discuss what is "real" and what is fabricated about reality TV, giving examples. What other aspects of our lives are presented as real, but are actually fabrications? (Or are there any that are NOT fabrications?)
2. As in the example of Crimp's *Attempts on Her Life* above, we all play different roles in our lives. How might people from various facets of your own life see you? Consider the many roles you play in our own life and list five (for example, daughter, student, girlfriend, best friend, employee). Next to each role, list three adjectives for each, describing how you think you are perceived in each role. (For example: employee – punctual, responsible, courteous.) Given the lists you've created,

is there one "real" you? How does this exercise relate to the postmodern concept of the loss of the real?

Next, choose one character from a play you are studying and conduct the same exercise, listing five social roles and three adjectives for each role. Do the roles clash? Are the clashes "realistic" or more fantastical (as in Crimp's play)? How do your findings relate to crystallization?

Form and content: the playwright's view

When interpreting a play, it makes sense to consider how and why the play is constructed from the playwright's perspective. How do nonlinear playwrights address structure when they teach students to write? Playwright/teachers Maria Irene Fornes, José Rivera, and David Crespy all address the issue of breaking from Aristotelian concepts of play structure.

Fornes, a Cuban-born playwright who first trained as a painter, came to playwriting after she saw a production of *Waiting for Godot* in France. Although she did not speak French, the production spoke volumes to her nonverbally and literally changed her outlook on life as well as her aspirations as an artist. Soon after, she moved to New York City and wrote her first play. When she first learned of the Aristotelian approach to play structure, Fornes recalls that she started laughing, reasoning that life did not follow a formula, nor should plays.

Fornes never dictates form to a playwriting class. She explains, "Don't try to tell a story.... You can't let structure destroy spontaneity. You have to allow yourself to have no idea where you're going. Be surprised by your own writing" (Svich 11). She encourages students to let an organic form emerge by accessing the subconscious mind, not the logical mind. She trains beginning playwrights by starting with yoga and physical exercises, helping students relax and become centered. Once she has awakened a student's inner sense, she begins a series of visualization exercises. Her exercises ask students to steer clear of predetermined paths and to remain in the moment, at times switching papers with each other, or adding an unexpected photograph or sentence into the mix of dialogue.

Like Fornes, playwright José Rivera steers his students away from dictating the structure of a play. Rivera uses exercises that emphasize the senses over the intellect and has students study plays by playwrights with a more visceral style, such as Sam Shephard, Caryl Churchill, Sarah Kane, and Mac Wellman. He tells students to think not of dramatic *structure,* but of *organization,* asking them to think geometrically: "Is this a pyramid in which you start off with one character and then introduce more and more until by the end of the play there are twenty people onstage? Or is this a circle in which the beginning and the end of the action are the same event?" (Herrington and Brian 49). Rivera also emphasizes that the organization should reflect upon the meaning of the play, that form and content should be similar. For example, a play about chaos could be chaotic in organization. Rivera's ideas remind us to take a closer look at the relationship of form and content. Are they parallel? Juxtaposed? Does one stand out over the other? In what way do they relate, and how does this relationship affect the play?

Like the playwrights above, playwright/teacher David Crespy seeks alternate methods to traditional playwriting with his advanced students, and uses dreams as a source of departure, influenced in part by the writings of theorist Bert O. States. He asks students to create a "dream cache," a physical container in which they keep their observations about their own dreams. Like Fornes, Crespy puts his students in a centered and meditative state in order to better access the subconscious mind. He also leads them through a series of exercises to recall and explore childhood dreams, recurring dreams, and recent dreams. Working from the dream cache, students use the magical transformations from dreams to influence their writing. Crespy states, "Luckily dream material is entirely subjective – meaning that there is no right or wrong.... Within each of these dreamplays specific dream transformation qualities can be explored – transfiguration, mutability, shifting landscapes, tremors of unreality or the bizarre or uncanny" (Crespy 9).

Given the propensity of these playwrights to abandon the logical mind, the artist reading a play should enter a similar state of mind in order to interpret the script. As you read a modern or postmodern play with a nontraditional form, do not be overly concerned about why the play suddenly shifts in a radical direction;

there may not be a logical reason. Too often we search for logical reasoning when the playwright is working from the unconscious and intuitive mind. It makes sense that using the meditative techniques found in Part I and awakening your own "inner eye" will help you find the key to understanding such plays.

EXERCISE: Form and content

1. After reading a nonlinear play straight through and recording your visceral responses (see Part I), return to the script and examine its organization. What comes first, and how do the pieces fit? Is it circular (beginning where it ends), a spiral, a pyramid, or does it take on some other form? Is there also a relationship between the form and content of the play, such as a chaotic idea being relayed through a chaotic form? Next, go back and mark any abrupt shifts in the play. They may be abrupt shifts/transformations in time, place, language, character, subject or style, for example. Are the shifts consistent throughout the play, or clustered? What effect do these shifts have on your visceral and intellectual responses to the work?

2. Try the following writing exercise:

   Sit down with a pad of paper or computer, a timer, and a magazine. Choose a fairy tale or fable you know well. Close your eyes and take a few deep breaths, letting the world around you fade. Conjure the world of the tale and the main character. Engage all your senses: sight, sound, touch, smell, and taste. Set a timer or alarm for 5 to 10 minutes, but try to ignore the timer as you begin writing a play version of the tale. When the timer goes off, open the magazine and point to a picture. Let this image abruptly change the scene going forward. Set the timer again and repeat the shift a second time, this time opening the magazine and randomly pointing to a word; immediately start using the word repeatedly, in unexpected ways, trying not to preplan, but to write freely. Read your resulting tale aloud with a partner. Did the shifts make the tale more interesting? Explain.

Visualizing structure: the landscape of a play and concept mapping

As we have seen above, contemporary playwrights often think outside of the traditions of causal/linear structure. Author and theorist Gertrude Stein, known for her avant-garde, minimalist writing and her support of modern art, described the structure of a play not as a line or a geometrical shape, but as a *landscape*. In her 1934 essay, "Play," Stein explained:

> A landscape is made up of things and people to be viewed in relation to each other. It doesn't have to come to you; you must discover for yourself what is there. This pictorial composition replaces dramatic action, emphasizing frontality and the frame, flatness and absence of perspective. The play is just there. It has no center. Whatever you find in it depends on your own way of looking. (Marranca 7)

Scholar Bonnie Marranca elaborates on Stein's idea of the play as a "cite of cultivation," writing, "Stein considers the relation of sight and sound to emotion and time, rather than story and action" (8). Although Stein was sometimes ridiculed at the time for her ideas and her writing, she foreshadowed the experimentation to come, both in modernist and postmodernist theories of symbol, reception, and the "loss of the real."

We can learn not only from theatre artists and theorists but from critics as well. According to Lowell Swortzell, *New York Times* theatre critic Walter Kerr "possessed the ability to capture a moment in the play or performance that epitomized the quality of the entire production." Swortzell argues that we can profit from Kerr's example by looking for "crossroads" and "defining moments" in plays (102). The metaphor of crossroads works well with Stein's conception of the landscape of the play. As you scan the vista of the play's landscape, look for crossroads. Extending the metaphor, are there also bridges, tunnels, mountains, valleys, or cliffs?

A related exercise that addresses the organization of the play is to create a concept map.[3] In *Classroom Assessment Techniques:*

A Handbook for College Teachers, Thomas A. Angelo and Patricia K. Cross provide a variety of frameworks for assessing student learning. They write: "Concept Maps are drawings or diagrams showing the mental connections that students make..." (197). Concept mapping is a useful tool in assessing your conceptualization of the play: how it moves, what patterns develop, and what (if anything) holds it together.

Two typical plot diagrams address the causal/linear plot and the episodic plot, the former usually depicted by a single line moving up through jagged steps of rising action (or complication) to a crisis point and back down through the resolution, and the latter depicted as circles – scenes or episodes – connected through a weblike pattern of relationships (see Figures 2.2 and 2.4).

Particularly when reading a play with a nonlinear plot, try creating your own diagram (or landscape, if you will). It may help to read the play aloud – to hear it in time and space, so to speak, in order to get a different perspective. Next, by constructing a visual diagram of the play, you reveal a personal, conceptual framework of understanding, as well as revealing gaps in understanding. This seemingly simple exercise draws on both intellectual and intuitive powers – a forge worth cultivating and exploring. Quite often my students create a diagram of a tree, drawing a metaphor of the roots, trunk, and branching pattern of a play. But how does the play conclude? (Or does it?) Do the various branch ends convey this conclusion? There may or may not be resolution, which the diagram must address.

As one example, while using this exercise to study David Henry Hwang's play, *M. Butterfly,* in an undergraduate literature class, a student of mine drew an oval-shaped spiral, which looked rather like the inside of a conch shell. He explained that the movement of the play seemed to be always turning back and inward, like a spiral coming to the center. I showed the class a photo from the Broadway production, which revealed a very similar scenic design by Eiko Ishioka, depicting a ramp that arched in a partial oval, turning inward around a central platform. The parallel with the student's diagram was striking, helping the class to see that the scenic design actually mirrored the structure and flow of the play itself, an exciting discovery.

EXERCISE: Concept mapping

1. Before drawing your map, consider the following questions:
   - How does the play move?
   - Does it unfold in one direction? Two? Many?
   - Is there a clear beginning, middle, and end?
   - Is there a single, pivotal crisis, or many crises?
   - Is the play, in fact, driven by plot, or held together by idea or some other element(s)?
   - How do the scenes or components connect together?
   - Is there a discernable pattern or patterns?
   - How does the action progress through time and space?
2. Now draw your visual map of the play and how it moves and connects. Do not be too concerned with what is "right" or "wrong," as this is your own interpretation of the play. Explain your map to a colleague and compare it with someone else's. Can you combine ideas with another person and create a new map that could communicate your collaborative ideas clearly?

Vocality and the playwright's voice

In describing *language playwrights,* Castagno writes, "The playwright is open to language in its widest sense, whether coded in a specific genre, found in another text, or produced by the linguistic impulses that unleash slang, unusual syntax, foreignisms, discourses, and so on" (2). He explains that plays may be *polyvocal,* having more than one narrative voice, or a voice that shifts unexpectedly in and out of a narrative (12). He gives examples of Len Jenkin's plays *My Uncle Sam* and *Dark Ride,* both of which shift the narrative to present a sense of disjuncture, allowing no single central character through whom to track the action. Castagno goes on to describe other unconventional linguistic devices, such as *captioning,* a framing device in which the speaker announces a shift of setting, or perhaps comments on a scene (think of Brecht's titled scenes or songs as a similar framing device).

Castagno also points to *carnivalesque* language, characters, and settings, giving a sense of "strange combinations, the overturning of expected norms, and the grotesque" (7). As an example, consider the following dialogue from Scene 27 of *Venus*, a play by Suzan-Lori Parks that includes a bizarre carnival world in which a nineteenth-century African woman is brought to Europe and billed as a sideshow attraction, The Venus Hottentot (see Figure III.1). The Mother-Showman calls out:

> Step right up come on come in
> Step inside come on come see
> The most lowly and unfortunate beings in Gods Universe:
> Mother-Showmans 9 Human Wonders will dazzle
> surprise intrigue horrify and disgust.
> The 9 lowest links in God's Great Chain of Being.
>
> THE CHORUS OF THE 8 HUMAN WONDERS.
> *Chain Chain Chain.* (40)

Later in the scene The Venus is presented to the crowd. Throughout the scene she has been bathing, with our attention veering from this private event to the public spectacle of the carnival. A spotlight comes up on the bathing Venus, instantly transporting her into the public venue. Actors who were portraying the other Human Wonders (sideshow performers) now gather around her, instantly becoming the Chorus of Spectators. Parks shifts to capital letters, giving The Mother-Showman the sense of a carnival barker:

> THE VENUS HOTTENTOT
> THE ONLY LIVING CREATURE OF HER KIND IN THE
>   WORLD
> STEPSISTER-MONKEY TO THE GREAT
> LOVE
> GODDESS
> AND ONLY ONE STEP UHWAY FROM YOU RIGHT NOW
> COME SEE THE HOT MISS HOTTENTOT
> STEP IN STEP IN
> HUR-RY! HUR-RY!
> HUR-RY! HUR-RY! (45)

Next, Parks takes the dialogue away completely, leaving us only with character names in a sequence. In her notes she explains that this structure represents more than a pause or rest; it is "a spell." Parks writes, "This is a place where the figures experience their pure true simple state. While no action or stage business is necessary, directors should fill this moment as they best see fit" (7). In the script, a spell creates what Parks calls an architectural look:

> THE VENUS.
> THE CHORUS OF THE SPECTATORS.
> THE VENUS.
> THE CHORUS OF THE SPECTATORS.
> THE VENUS.
> THE CHORUS OF THE SPECTATORS.
> THE VENUS.
> THE CHORUS OF THE SPECTATORS.
>
> *(Rest.)*
>
> THE VENUS.
> Oh, God:
> unloved.
> *(Rest.)*
>
> THE NEGRO RESSURECTIONIST.
> Footnote #3:
> Historical Extract. Category: Literary. From Robert Chambers's *Book of Days:*
> [The actor proceeds to quote from Chambers's *Book of Days,* changing narrative voice.] (46)

The first clue to Parks's postmodern approach is the lack of standard punctuation, grammar, spelling, and capitalization. Words on the page become poetic verse, with lines broken at will. Repeatedly, character names are listed on the page – as above with THE VENUS and THE CHORUS OF SPECTATORS – with no dialogue following. At other times, there may be repeated words, counting, odd slang ("Diggidy-diggidy-diggidy-dawg") or sounds depicted by letters. The theatricality is overt, not only though the language, but through double casting and sudden shifts in time, place, and action. Some scenes alternate between the carnival and an autopsy of The Venus, filled with medical jargon. Structurally, the play has numbered scenes, but the numbers count down rather than up, from 31 to 1. As with the shifting narrative, the chronology is only loosely held together. In *Plays Onstage: An Anthology,* editors Ronald Wainscott and Kathy Fletcher reflect on the relationship of form and content:

> The play at times seems to become the form that it deconstructs; it doesn't just present the sideshow, the freak show, but often imitates it. The language is alternately schematic and poetic, emblematic and abbreviated, profane and clinical. Parks is fond of modern musical forms and often uses riffs and snatches of music both literally and figuratively. (527)

Figure III.1 *Venus,* by Suzan-Lori Parks, directed by Jason Neulander at Salvage Vanguard Theater

Source: Photo by Sarah Bork Hamilton.

Clearly Parks has her own voice, and it breaks with our traditional conception of sentence structure and narrative. In *Writing Down the Bones*, Natalie Goldberg explains why the writer should break with traditional syntax in creative writing. "We think in sentences, and the way we think is the way we see. If we think in the structure subject/verb/direct-object, then that is how we form our world. By cracking open that syntax, we release energy and are able to see the world afresh from a new angle" (62). Through Parks's fractured, collage-like text, we are transported not to a realistic world, but to the unique world of the play, which is continuously being revealed. Much like interpreting a Rorschach inkblot or an abstract painting, our minds try to synthesize the information and create something meaningful. In perceiving and interpreting, we screen the incoming sensations through our personal experiences, knowledge base, biases, values, and tastes. We form some kind of personal meaning, jumping the gaps and filling in as needed. The world of the play provokes us and challenges us to make those creative leaps.

How does a director approach a script by Suzan-Lori Parks, a playwright who relies as much on image and sound as she does on text? I asked this question of Liz Diamond, who directed many of Parks's early works in their original productions. Initially, she and Parks worked together, sometimes with Parks reading the script aloud and Diamond asking questions. By listening to the play, images and ideas emerged, and Diamond took these into rehearsal and played with the text as a musical score of sorts, finding the rhythm as well as the poetry (Fliotsos and Vierow 147). In a separate interview, Diamond states, "To hell with subtext.…The action that's on the language and in the language, the way it operates in your body and on your tongue, tells you how to play it" (Anderman N1). Reading a play aloud, therefore, can be an excellent way to liberate you from the mindset of literary analysis. Moving the body intuitively with the words can also unlock fresh interpretations, but performers must be willing to work from instinct and not from a stance of having all the answers or understanding the play intellectually first.

EXERCISE: New language playwriting

Select a script from a nonlinear play, using one of the playwrights previously listed or one of your choosing. (*Tip: playwright Charles Mee's plays are free and available on the internet on his website; simply search his name.*) Form a small group and follow these steps:

1. Before meeting as a group, read the script silently to yourself and take notes on your visceral responses (see Part I). Also note your initial questions and/or what confuses you about the play. It may be helpful to know some basic contextual information about the play and its subject, but refrain from conducting extensive research at this point.
2. Before getting too far into your analytical mind, meet with a group and read the play aloud, again noting your responses as you listen. What new ideas and observations surfaced from hearing the play?
3. Select a single scene from the play and get the group up on its feet. (It will be helpful to have at least one observer.) Conduct a few warm-ups to get the group moving and working together, then read the scene aloud, using the rhythm, sounds, and patterns of the language to influence bodily movement. This is free-form improvisation and may look more like dance or abstract movement. It need not be "realistic" or psychologically based. How do the performers' bodies react to the shifts in the text? How do the words, sounds, and rhythms "play" the body as an instrument? Look for other interpretations. For example, do body positions change if narrative shifts?
4. After discussing the steps above, sit down with your group and compose a description of how language works in your particular play, referring back to the text in this section (and Castagno's book, if possible). Be prepared to share your findings with others.

Interpreting the de-centered script: Key moments, lateral thinking, and exquisite pressure

While there is no one method to interpreting a nonlinear text, we can learn much from studying the methods of directors who routinely interpret or create such scripts in production. The terms below come from directors Anne Bogart and Tina Landau, though other groups and directors use similar concepts and terms.

Key moments

Whether reading the play aloud or to yourself on the page, one way to focus on your interpretation of the play is to open your eyes to key or climactic moments, memorable moments that stand out. You need not understand what they mean in a first reading; perhaps it is the questions that are raised that will provoke you.

Various artists have pointed to these key moments in different ways. In Stanislavski's action analysis, he asks artists to look for three major climaxes, found in the beginning, middle, and end of each play. However, in modern and postmodern plays, there may be little definition of these Aristotelian concepts of progression. As we saw in Part II, the three climaxes are only one aspect of action analysis. Looking for the seed of the play, the sequence of internal and external events, and the super-objective are all equal parts of the puzzle. My own students have found action analysis to be a helpful tool in interpreting nonlinear texts, although the pieces of the puzzle may not easily fall into place because of a play's unusual structure.

In *The Viewpoints Book* (2005), directors Anne Bogart and Tina Landau write not of climaxes, but of "what *floats up*" (181) in the mind – a more abstract notion, which is related to the idea of a climactic moment. The premise is simple: after reading a play or watching a performance, key moments float up to the top of your mind. If you are able to submerge yourself into the world of the play while reading, pay attention to your visceral responses. Pause afterwards, breathe, and notice what floats up. What are you left with? Words? Images? Actions? A sense of foreboding? It can take many forms. There is no prescribed number of moments, and they need not be divided as beginning, middle, and end. The more important question is: *what* are the moments and *why* and *how* do these moments engage you? Dig more deeply to discover how these key moments affect the relationships in the play, its progression, and its meaning to you.

Case study: Viewpoints

Viewpoints is movement-based training that allows performers to experience the text through different lenses, literally through different points of view, with particular attention to time, space, and relationship.[4] Director-auteur Anne Bogart and her colleagues at the SITI Company have developed Viewpoints for actors, expanding dancer/choreographer Mary Overlie's original six Viewpoints to nine Physical Viewpoints: Spatial Relationship, Kinesthetic Response, Shape, Gesture, Repetition, Architecture, Tempo, Duration, and Topography.

When learning Viewpoints, performers train in one Viewpoint at a time through a variety of exercises. This allows them to gain a bodily understanding of each Viewpoint before combining them or working with text or music. Once in rehearsal, the Viewpoints provide a vocabulary – a shorthand of sorts – for the physical realm of a scene. For example, if the director asks for attention to Kinesthetic Response, the performer complies by reacting more specifically to the movement of other performers (or objects) around him/her. If the director suggests Architecture, the performer responds viscerally to the architecture of the working space, bringing awareness to floors, ceilings, walls, surfaces, corners, niches, and so on.

Viewpoints can be used when interpreting any text to stage, including deconstructing the text, as well as in the creation of devised (original) work. With its concentration on physical response, Viewpoints helps performers de-center the text, a valuable tool in exploring postmodern work. Because the Physical Viewpoints are based in movement, they need to be seen or performed through the body to be truly understood. Here we can only approach Viewpoints training as a collaborative, improvisatory philosophy, to be physically explored through your own training.[5]

Lateral thinking

One of the benefits of improvised physical work is solving the puzzle of the play collaboratively. Bogart and Landau believe in working off one another in small groups, using what they call lateral thinking (156). In first posing questions and brainstorming ideas (through words, images, music, objects, movement, or virtually anything), lateral thinking refers to others riffing off those ideas. By creating new collaborative pathways unavailable to the individual, the realm of the possible cracks wide open. They write:

> Can the artistic process be collaborative? Can a group of strong-minded individuals *together* ask what the play or project *wants*, rather than depending upon the hierarchical domination of one person? ... Can we resist proclaiming "what it is" long enough to authentically ask: "What is it?" (Bogart and Landau 18)

Actors, directors, and designers can become trapped in their own expectations of a role or of a play. Actors often complain, "my character would never do that," in part because they project their own attitudes and opinions onto the character. Directors and designers may also have a knee-jerk reaction, thinking, "my production (or design) would never include that" (Bogart and Landau 125). While first impressions of a role or a design are vitally important, they should not be the sole impetus for the final result. Director Peter Brook writes that the ideas that are formed before rehearsals begin run the risk of imposing "cast-iron forms," and that collaboration requires a balancing "between what must be prepared in advance and what can safely be left open" (126). Bogart and Landau also encourage us away from close-mindedness, advocating "finding more unexpected choices, remaining open to what happens and what stirs you, rather than what you originally thought should and should not" (125). It is important for a collaborative group to stick to the central questions being posed, but to hang loose enough to explore possibilities.

Exquisite pressure

Blurring the line between process and product, Bogart and Landau apply what they call exquisite pressure, giving groups just enough time to create something that is repeatable, but not enough time to judge or second-guess their choices (138). Lookingglass Theatre in Chicago teaches a similar technique, asking groups of performers to create a tableau in about four seconds flat. There is no time for discussion: exquisite pressure is improvisation and raw instinct at work. Directors and teachers already realize the benefits of this technique from experience. In my own graduate-level script interpretation class, composed of both actors and designers, I ask students to read an unpublished, postmodern play. We discuss our initial, visceral reactions, then get up on our feet – before we succumb to our analytical minds – and move to a rehearsal room. Under strict time constraints, groups must stage a scene based on their instincts, using any masks and odd props that I bring with me. With exquisite pressure they are forced to privilege *creating* the scene over *discussing* it. They riff off each other's ideas (lateral thinking), letting one movement, sound, or visual image spark the next. After performing the scenes for each other, we discuss the spectators' reactions before addressing the performers' intent. Working from a complex and abstract text with this simple method of getting up and creating from impulse can be the most rewarding, creative, and eye-opening class of the semester. The previous discussion of our responses to the scene pale in comparison to our experiential responses, and students who initially think they had no connection to the script find themselves engaged by new theatrical possibilities. This method can be particularly effective with scenes that don't seem to make sense on a first reading. Find other dimensions of expressing the play. Postmodern theory reminds us that the text is only a jumping off point and should not outweigh theatrical methods of communicating.

Questions for application

Broad questions are preferred in reflexive inquiry because they allow for freedom of discovery. This does not imply a lack of rigor.

Philip Taylor reminds us that "reflective practitioner researchers often raise more questions than solutions" (53). When you don't yet have a solution, formulate a specific statement of a question that remains, and keep working. Often revelations come later in the process of production.

- Why or how is your play nonlinear? Is it also postmodern? Explain.
- Do you detect a hybrid plot construction? for example, does the play have a linear/causal plot in some sections with deviations in other sections?
- What comes first in the play, and how does this relate to the end? What do you consider its organizing principle? (Think geometrically.)
- What is the relationship between form and content? For example, does a scene about chaos suddenly become chaotic in the way it is constructed?
- How can you draw the play as a landscape? Look for hills, valleys, plateaus, bridges, crossroads, and tunnels.
- How might the play be depicted in a concept map? (See preliminary questions in the exercise Creating a concept map)
- What are the key moments in the play that float to the top of your mind?
- *Why* and *how* did these key moments engage you? How do the key moments affect the given relationships in the play, its progression, and/or its meaning? Do they provide crossroads in the landscape of the play?
- How would you describe the vocality of the play? Is there one clear narrative voice, or do the voices change? What special attributes of language flavor the vocal texture of the play?
- Read the play aloud, either alone or with a partner. How do rhythm, tempo, and mood come alive with the reading? What floats up?
- Apply exquisite pressure. Select one scene and with a group, put it on its feet. Play. Explore. Take risks. Work off one another through instinct, using lateral thinking.

Notes

1. In *Postdramatic Theatre* (2006, published in German in 1996), Hans-Thies Lehmann chooses the term *postdramatic* to reflect scripts that no longer focus on traditional concepts of dramatic action and characterization. For example, British playwrights Martin Crimp and Sara Kane have written plays (such as *Attempts on Her Life* and *4:48 Psychosis*, respectively) consisting of lines with no characters and no particular plot. The director, performers, and designers must find the play themselves, with plenty of latitude for interpretation. Whereas these plays are usually assigned the label of *postmodern*, Lehmann finds the term *postdramatic* more to the point (Lehmann 2006: 1).
2. As another example, television comedian Steven Colbert coined the term "truthiness" on *The Colbert Report* (October 17, 2005), adding his own twist to our fabricated notions of truth or reality. With "truthiness," there is no real truth, only that which seems true if given the right "spin." The American Dialect Society named "truthiness" the Word of the Year in 2005, and Merriam-Webster included it as one of their Words of the Year for 2006.
3. This description of concept mapping is previously published in my article, "From Script Analysis to Script Interpretation: Valorizing the Intuitive" in *Theatre Topics*, 19.2 (September 2009): 153–63.
4. Though we can identify specific Viewpoints, there is no single definition of what Viewpoints means; instead, the term is used in a variety of ways. We can discuss Viewpoints holistically, individually, as a process, as a philosophy, and as a language, among other things.
5. The SITI Company leads workshops on Viewpoints, and it is not uncommon for colleges and arts institutions to incorporate Viewpoints training in their theatre and dance curricula. For further information, see the SITI Company webpage at www.siti.org.

Sources and further study

Anderman, Joan. "Her Battlefield is a Woman's Soul." *Boston Globe*, November 22, 1998.

Angelo, Thomas A. and Patricia K. Cross. *Classroom Assessment Techniques: A Handbook for College Teachers*. 2nd ed. San Francisco: Jossey-Bass, 1993.

Barry, Peter. *Beginning Theory*. Manchester: Manchester University Press, 1995.

Bogart, Anne and Tina Landau. *The Viewpoints Book: A Practical Guide to Viewpoints and Composition*. New York: TCG, 2005.

Brook, Peter. *There Are No Secrets: Thoughts on Acting and Theatre*. London: Methuen, 1995.

Castagno, Paul C. *New Playwriting Strategies*. London: Routledge, 2001.

Crespy, David A. "Dreamwork for Playwriting." Paper. Annual International Conference on Fine and Performing Arts, Athens Institute for Education and Research. Athens, Greece, June 2010.

Crimp, Martin. *Attempts on Her Life*. London: Faber and Faber, 1997.

Fliotsos, Anne. "Valorizing the Intuitive: From Script Analysis to Script Interpretation." *Theatre Topics*, 19.2 (September 2009): 153–63.

Fliotsos, Anne and Wendy Vierow. *American Women Stage Directors of the Twentieth Century*. Urbana, IL: University of Illinois Press, 2008.

Goldberg, Natalie. *Writing Down the Bones*. Boston, MA: Shambhala, 1986.

Haring-Smith, Tori. "Dramaturging Non-Realism: Creating a New Vocabulary." *Theatre Topics*, 13.1 (March 2003): 45–54.

Herrington, Joan and Crystal Brian (eds.). *Playwrights Teach Playwriting*. Lyme, NH: Smith & Kraus, 2006.

Lehmann, Hans-Thies. *Postdramatic Theatre*. Trans. Karen Jürs-Munby. London: Routledge, 2006.

Marranca, Bonnie. *Ecologies of Theater: Essays at Century Turning*. Baltimore: Johns Hopkins University Press, 1996.

O'Reilley, Mary Rose. *The Peaceable Classroom*. Portsmouth, NH: Heinemann, 1993.

Parks, Suzan-Lori. *Venus*. New York: Theatre Communications Group, 1998.

Richardson, Laurel. "Writing: A Method of Inquiry." *Handbook of Qualitative Research*. Ed. Norman K. Denizin and Yvonna S. Lincoln. Thousand Oaks, CA: Sage, 1994. 516–29.

Russolo, Luigi. "The Art of Noise." Trans. Victoria Nes Kirby. In Michael Kirby, *Futurist Performance*. New York: PAJ, 1986.

Svich, Caridad. "The Legacy of Maria Irene Fornes: A Collection of Impressions and Exercises." *PAJ*, 31.3 (September 2009): 1–32.

Swortzell, Lowell. "History as Drama/Drama as History: The Case for Historical Reconstruction as a Research Paradigm." *Researching Drama and Arts Education: Paradigms and Possibilities*. Ed. Philip Taylor. London: Routledge Falmer, 1996, 97–104.

Taylor, Philip, ed. *Researching Drama and Arts Education: Paradigms and Possibilities*. London: Falmer, 1996.

Turner, Cathy and Synne Behrndt. *Dramaturgy and Performance.* New York: Palgrave Macmillan, 2008.

Wainscott, Ronald and Kathy Fletcher. *Plays Onstage: An Anthology.* Boston, MA: Pearson, 2006.

Whitmore, Jon. *Directing Postmodern Theater: Shaping Signification in Performance.* Ann Arbor, MI: University of Michigan Press, 1994.

Wright, Michael. *Playwriting Master Class: The Personality of Process and the Art of Rewriting.* 2nd ed. Newburyport, MA: Focus, 2010.

IV

Responding to the Script

On finding a path to understanding

In the introduction of this book I argue that both subjective and objective approaches to the script are valuable and necessary. As demonstrated in Part III, modern and postmodern construction is unique, requiring us to deviate from traditional analysis. In other words, when interpreting a script, you need to choose the right tool for the job.

Despite the best efforts of any teacher or author, there is no single, foolproof way to approach a text. One reason is the variety of scripts, and another the variety within the individuals reading the text. Just as we all have different learning styles and artistic approaches, we eventually discover what works for us and what does not. Master director and theorist Eugenio Barba posits, "No true ABC exists. Everyone has his or her own and has to invent his or her own first steps. In art, whenever we find a rule, a principle or an axiom, we are also aware that – in the measure in which it is true – its opposite is also true" (quoted in Zarrilli xiii). Simply being open-minded to alternatives is not enough, though it is a good first step. Barba explains that we sometimes stumble into our understanding, writing, "At times, however much we may regret it, a vague, confused, and superstitious attitude may be as beneficial on a practical level as a scientifically based awareness" (xiv). The unknown and unexplained present a mystery in the work, and not every question must be answered before going into production, though a path of inquiry – knowing what the questions are and how to approach those questions – is a necessary starting point. The landscape, or architecture, of the play is a site of discovery, to be explored through the process of both reading and creating the piece.

Consider the process of interpreting a script as you would going on a voyage. Two travelers, A and Z, present two opposite extremes of taking that voyage. Traveler A likes to plan her trip entirely, researching the area, choosing the sights to see, studying the history, finding the perfect hotels and restaurants with all the best reviews, and planning virtually every hour of her itinerary. This traveler may have a smooth trip, but the site of discovery has likely become the internet, books, and other research tools rather than the landscape of the place itself. Traveler A wants to depart on her voyage with the security of knowing all the answers, completely in control. In contrast, traveler Z is a free spirit, following his intuition and exploring each sight as he encounters it. He has done little to no preplanning, hoping the trip will take on a life of its own. This traveler may get stuck in a rotten hotel (if he finds one at all) and miss the traditional tourist destinations, but he will have unique experiences along the way. He will likely get lost in a sketchy part of town, perhaps putting himself in danger. Traveler Z's site of discovery is each place in each lived moment.

Is one trip better than another, or more successful? Certainly both have pitfalls. The trips could be to the same place at the same time, but the voyage of discovery and the interpretation of the place will be quite different. Most of us opt for something between the two extremes: having an overall plan of action and preparation, while giving ourselves room to explore and follow our instincts. Unlike the travelers in our scenario, we are not alone on our voyage to production; others rely on us in a collaborative team and therefore we must be prepared. That being said, we need to find the balance (the *yin–yang*, if you will) of preparation and discovery in the moment.

Considering the audience and occasion

Where or when will you have to present your response to the script? If you are a director or designer, it may be your first design meeting, or even at an interview for a design job. If you are an actor, you may be asked to reflect on the script at the start of rehearsals, but you may also be asked questions as early as auditions or callbacks. Even if you are not asked to make a formal presentation about the script, you should come to interviews, auditions, meetings, and rehearsals prepared to discuss your response to the script, both intuitively and analytically. Bring something to the collaborative production process as an interpretive artist. How did the play work on you, provoking your reactions? How did you work on it, discovering its structure, organization, and what makes it work? What images, sounds, objects, or other associations come to mind? What questions linger? As a traveler going on this voyage of discovery, what is your plan going forward? What are the plans of the others on your voyage, and how will you travel together, as a team?

If you are writing a paper or making a formal presentation, you will clearly need a more defined, formal path for your journey. In a class setting, your professor will likely provide specific guidelines. Whether you are presenting as a student or a working artist (or both), remember to consider your audience and the goal of your presentation. When in doubt, ask what kind of information is expected of you and adapt as needed.

EXERCISE: Outlining your presentation[1]

While no two presentations are alike, below I summarize the elements for a *possible* presentation or paper. I hope the sections of this book and the questions at the end of each section will provoke further thought as you prepare your responses. Avoid simply answering the questions one by one; rather construct a cohesive report of your interpretation of the play. Tell your audience what type of interpretation you are conducting, your path of investigation, and why this path is appropriate for your particular play.

I. *Intuitive and contemplative responses*
  A. Emotional, physical (senses), spiritual, and intellectual responses
  B. How/when these responses changed throughout the script
  C. What you bring of yourself and your culture into the response (memories, experiences, biases, morals, values, etc.)
  D. How your response changed from initial to subsequent readings
  E. Associational materials (images, art, scent, color, objects, sounds, tactile responses)
  F. Reflective constructions: ideographs, poster images, collages, tableaux
II. *Action analysis (as a separate analysis, or inserted into Analysis of elements – below, with areas suggested in brackets)*
  A. Sequence of external events [Plot]
  B. Review of facts [World of the play]
  C. Seed of the play [Idea]
  D. Sequence of internal events, linked to the seed [Idea]
  E. Theme [Idea]
  F. Super-objective [Character]
  G. Through-action and counter through-action [Plot]
III. *Analysis of elements (drawing from Aristotelian, Stanislavski-based, nontraditional, or some combination, as best matches your script)*
  A. World of the play
    1. given circumstances (the who, what, when, and where): consider time, space/locale, society/culture, governance/politics, economics, spirituality, transformative or nonrealistic qualities
    2. background story leading up to start of play
    3. genre (comedy, tragedy, melodrama, drama, farce)
  B. Plot
    1. type (linear/causal, multi-linear, episodic, hybrid, or other)[2]

- structure/organization (for causal/linear plots, include exposition, inciting incident, rising action, crisis, climax, falling action, resolution)
- diagram and description: concept map or landscape
- relationship between form and content

2. scene breakdowns (if required): units and beats
3. statement of through-action and counter-through action

C. Character
1. identify central character (protagonist), opposing character (antagonist), ensemble, or other approach[3]
2. functions (foil, raisonneur, confidante, chorus, norm character, stereotype, multivocal character, narrator, etc.)
3. facts and evidence about characters (consider bias of source)
4. super-objective of central character(s)

D. Idea
1. title of play
2. idea as revealed in crisis and resolution of the play
3. aphorism, or overt statement of idea from dialogue
4. recurring motifs (possible use of pattern)
5. concise statement of the seed and theme

E. Language
1. style: verse, prose, narrative, monologues, asides, silence, overlapping dialogue, simultaneous dialogue, implications of punctuation
2. character differentiation: dialect, jargon, rhythm, rhyme, slang, aphorisms, clichés, metaphors, questions, commands, length of sentences
3. modern and postmodern: carnivalesque, repetition, pattern, silence, framing, self-reference, polyvocal, nonsense, juxtaposition

F. Music (aural elements)
1. music and sound required or referenced

        2. musicality of language (tempo, rhythm, tone, mood, etc.)

        3. aural emphasis: how does sound contribute to the play?

    G. Spectacle (visual elements)

        1. scale of spectacle and effects required or referenced (If large or overt spectacle is called for, to what end?)

        2. visual metaphor or iconography in the play

        3. visual emphasis: how does spectacle contribute to the play?

    H. Other elements (scent or tactile, for example)

    I. Leading element: does one element overshadow the others? (Is the play driven by character? By idea? Consider leading your discussion with the driving element.)

IV. *Contextual research (only alluded to in this book)*

    A. The playwright (his biography, his works, and how they all relate)

    B. The period (for both the setting and the writing of the play)

    C. The culture (socioeconomic, religious, education, government, etc.)

    D. Major issues or historical facts and figures in the play

    E. Production reviews (successes and pitfalls of past productions)

    F. Literary critiques and other critical analysis

    G. Style of the play (and/or production; see below)

V. *Conclusion: preproduction interpretation of the script*

    A. Summary: the heart of the play (what makes it work)

    B. Consideration of modern audience versus audience of the play's period (Will a modern audience still relate? What are possible stumbling blocks or bridges for the audience?)

    C. Your plan of action or inquiry, based on your investigation and the director's vision

    D. Remaining questions to investigate in rehearsal or preproduction

Style and critical lenses

Mirriam-Webster's dictionary defines *style* as "a distinctive manner of expression" or "a particular manner or technique by which something is done, created, or performed." First and foremost, the play may be written in a particular style (French neoclassical, symbolist, realistic, etc.), requiring that you study that movement's underlying theory as well as how the plot, character, idea, language, aural, and visual components are all stylized. Remember that one element may overshadow the others. For example, in a symbolist play, the atmosphere created through visual and aural elements overshadows the other elements, for the symbolists wished the audience to enter the world of the inner mind and spirit. Characters are metaphorical and undeveloped rather than psychologically complex, and the action of the plot may be fairly static.[4]

In addition to particular stylistic movements, you should consider the individual style of the playwright. For example, as we saw in Part II, David Mamet is known for his stylized language, such as the staccato-like rhythms of his plays, among other aspects. Bear in mind that like Picasso, who had several distinctive stylistic periods, a playwright may move through various styles within his or her body of work. Eugene O'Neill, for instance, experimented with expressionism in *The Emperor Jones* and *The Hairy Ape,* though the majority of his plays are realistic or naturalistic.

A further stylistic concern for theatre artists includes the director's vision for the production. It is possible that your director or producer will ask you to view the play through a particular critical lens. For instance, you might be asked to work on a feminist deconstruction of a classic American drama. Likewise, you may be asked to bring expressionistic elements into the design and performance of a play. It is not uncommon for contemporary plays to be based in realism, but have moments that depart from realism: surreal or magical moments, often referred to as "magical realism." Craig Lucas's play *Prelude to a Kiss* displays this quality when an old man observing a wedding party kisses the bride and their souls exchange. Pinpointing this shift of style in a hybrid play is critical.

Addressing the complex issues of style and critical stance are beyond the scope of this book; you must engage in outside research. Though the internet has a vast array of materials, sights, and sounds that are literally at your fingertips, it should not be your only source of information. Authoritative sources such as books and scholarly articles will bring some balance and depth to your research. There are hundreds of possible books to help you along the way; a few are recommended here as reference material. Full citations are given in Sources and further readings at the end of this section.

- *History*: A basic theatre history textbook will present an overview of the period and style you are researching and therefore provides a good starting point. Oscar G. Brockett's *History of the Theatre* (2008), coauthored by Franklin J. Hildy, has been a standard in the field for decades, though there are many others.
- *Literary styles and criticism* are well explained in Peter Barry's *Beginning Theory: An Introduction to Literary and Cultural Theory* (2009) as well as John Gassner and Edward Quinn's *The Reader's Encyclopedia of World Drama* (2002).
- *Acting styles*: For specific information on acting styles, consult Robert Barton's *Style for Actors* (2009), John Harrop and Sabin Epstein's *Acting with Style* (1999), or Jerry Crawford's *Acting: In Person and in Style* (1994).
- *Theatrical/cultural styles*: Douglas A. Russell's *Period Style for the Theatre* (1987) remains a good starting point for artistic, cultural, and theatrical styles up to the late twentieth century.
- *Visual art:* Any number of art and design books will also be helpful, such as Anthony Janson's *Janson's History of Art* (2006) and Laurie Schneider Adams's *A History of Western Art* (2004).

It benefits researchers to get a grounding in general sources, such as those above, then move to more specific sources, such as journal articles. An excellent online database for searching journals is *The International Bibliography of Theatre and Dance*. Also helpful is the *MLA International Bibliography*, although literature is more heavily covered than performance and production. Consult with a reference librarian for your specific research needs.

Contextual considerations: global cultures

It is not enough to consider the script as an entity unto itself. We must also include the audience and the creative team in our study of script interpretation. As artists and practitioners we may work in international festivals, in cross-cultural productions, and with translated scripts. Even when working in our home countries, we work with people of different cultural backgrounds and present our work to diverse audiences. Clearly, cultural interpretations play a role in our interpretation of art. We must continually think of ourselves not only as artists and reflective practitioners, but as ethnographers, searching to understand how culture and language play upon our perceptions.

We live in an era of globalization, an oft-used buzzword referring to the intercommunication and interconnectedness of cultures around the world. In the twenty-first century it is not enough to privilege our own way of seeing things. As artists, we must also be explorers, striving to see through the eyes of others. Many cultures deviate from the neo-positivist slant of our own. For example, Dutch film director Rolf de Heer worked with Aboriginal people in Australia when making his film *Ten Canoes* (2006). He documents his experience in a DVD extra feature, *The Bandala and the Bark Canoes*. Noticing fundamental differences in cultures, he states, "The cosmology of the Yolgna people is an entirely different cosmology than ours. The universe is a different place. The way of thinking is therefore different, and the language, apart from being structurally different, describes different things. Ours is a language of classification and categorization. Theirs is a language of connection and unity; everything is all one." In order to reflect the culture of the Bandala, de Heer had to recognize these critical cultural and linguistic differences.

Arthur Miller experienced a transformation of his own when directing *Death of A Salesman* in Beijing in 1983, well before capitalistic tendencies had infiltrated Chinese culture. He anticipated a number of obstacles as he considered the cultural differences. How would the actors and audience relate to this very American play? Would they understand the Western practice of door-to-door sales or the concept of life insurance in communist China? Would they understand what drives Willy to suicide? Could they relate to the American ideals of individualism? Fortunately, Miller's lead actor also served as the interpreter and translator for the text, and it was through him that Miller was able to effect understanding among the cast, many of whom were determined to "play American." With the potential for disaster, Miller ultimately found his way into the heart and mind of the Chinese audience. In particular, it related to the struggle for harmony within the family. Willy's dogged fight to provide for his family and live with dignity resonated greatly with a Chinese public that had lived through the horrors of the Cultural Revolution of the 1960s and 1970s.

In his memoire, *Salesman in Beijing,* Miller writes not only of the cultural obstacles, but the basic issue of translating the script into a language that differs in its fundamental structure. Like de Heer, he found a different cultural ideology reflected in the language. Miller writes:

> It is phenomenally difficult to translate literary works into Chinese, although somewhat easier the other way. It is not merely the totally different syntax, if that word even applies to Chinese, but perhaps more fundamentally the Chinese tendency to speak in images, and better yet, images of startling density and complexity. "I don't like to rush through an art exhibition" becomes "I don't like to ride past pictures on a fast horse." ... In comparison, everyday English seems unpoetic in this metaphoric sense, more fact-bound. (101)

Director and educator Richard Trousdell reminds us to always consider the situation when interpreting a play, writing, "Often ... time and culture block our empathy with the basic human situations of classic or foreign material. In such cases, directors sometimes find it necessary to 'translate' or 'update' a play's context into a familiar vernacular" (36). When reading a script, be aware of your own knowledge (or lack thereof) of the period and culture being represented. Clearly, contextual research is needed for any play, but considering cultural traditions and mores is important before making snap judgments. Our own moral sense may give us a knee-jerk reaction; we may find the play sexist, racist, or otherwise offensive. In some cases the script is simply oblique, or at odds with our worldview. For example, we may not understand the code of honor that dictates a marriage between two characters who do not love each other in a play such as *Life is a Dream*.[5] Fully investigate the period and culture as an ethnographer would, and try to consider the play from the perspective of the play's original audience. As theatre practitioners, we must ultimately make decisions for our own audiences and our own time – what lines may be cut or altered, for example, if it is a play out of copyright. However, before taking an axe to the script, be sure to know where its heart lies and what made it beat in its own day and age.

Allowing for change in rehearsal and production

The initial phase of interpreting a script is an important starting point for your work in production, a road map of sorts. However, as you begin your journey, be willing to go "off road" and explore new options during the development and rehearsal process. Your initial script interpretation provides impressions and factual information; it provides you with a list of qualities about the play, your initial responses, and questions for further investigation in production, but it is a beginning, not an ending. For example, actors may prefer to leave their initial script interpretation at the rehearsal door (to get "out of their heads," so to speak), starting a second phase of discovery with fresh eyes. You may wish to come back to your initial impressions at a later point, to find the connecting tissue from one process of discovery to another. As you embark on this journey of discovery, remind yourself to search for new possibilities.

Questions for application

- Who is your audience and what is the purpose of your paper or presentation?
- What type of analysis or interpretation best suit the script at hand and why? Are you including both subjective and objective investigations? Why or why not?
- How can you best create a personal statement (in any media) which best communicates your reaction to and understanding of this script? Consider the exercises throughout the book and think of aides that may help you express your associations (taste, touch, sight, smell, scent).
- When looking at the sample outline, remember that not all elements have equal weight. Does one element (plot, character, idea, language, music, spectacle) take precedence? Consider addressing the elements in the order of their importance.
- What is the style of the play? Of the playwright? How would you describe the artistic vocabulary of this work? Does it employ more than one style?
- Consider the director's vision for the script. Is there a specific critical lens you are using in production (highlighting, for example, race, gender, class, or a specific political viewpoint)? How is this addressed in your interpretation?
- What outside sources do you need to consult for contextual research? Work from general to specific sources.
- How do your own cultural traditions and mores influence your reading of this play?
- How does your research into the period and culture of the play inform your understanding? Consider the period/culture both of the play's setting and of the playwright, if they differ.
- If you are considering altering the script in any way (such as cutting lines or characters, altering the plot, or reorganizing the scenes), be sure that the script is out of copyright or get permission from whomever holds the rights. What is at the heart of the play, and how will your adaptation help you relate the play to a modern audience?
- What questions still remain as you go into the next phase of production?

Notes

1. Aristotle's six elements comprise a large part of Section 3 of this outline, but do not presuppose that this must be Aristotelian analysis. Rather, the element names are used as a frame for examination, and you must find the method of interpretation that works best for your play within each element. Options for non-traditional forms are suggested for consideration within this framework.

2. The hardest part of play analysis for beginners is often determining the architecture of the play itself. Is this a linear/causal, episodic, circular, a hybrid, or some other unique structure? Modern playwrights tend to be eclectic, mixing linear, episodic, or any number of structures. Remember that the chronological order of events does not necessarily mean the plot is linear/causal, rather one scene must trigger the next. A hybrid play may also start with one structure, then veer from the original path.

3. Modernist and post-modernist characters will likely fall outside of the "traditional" realm of characters, which are psychological constructs. See also sources below in the section marked *Style,* as well as Paul Castagno's *New Playwriting Strategies*, Chapter 4: "The Theatricality of Character."

4. For example, in Maurice Maeterlinck's one act play, *Interior*, a sense of foreboding and anticipation dominate the play, though there is little overt action. An old man and a stranger stand outside in the night, watching a family through the window of their house. They discuss how to inform the family that their daughter's body has been found. The driving force is tone or mood, depicted through the visual and aural elements: a sense of darkness, isolation (the family is observed from outside), and foreboding as we await the inevitable conclusion that will change their lives.

5. This particular example stems from José Rivera's 1998 play *Sueño*, an adaptation of Calderón's classic Spanish play, *La Vida Es Sueño*. Rivera gives an informative description of his process of adaptation for a modern audience in the introduction to the play.

Sources and further study

Adams, Laurie Schneider. *A History of Western Art*. 4th ed. New York: McGraw-Hill, 2004.

Barry, Peter. *Beginning Theory: An Introduction to Literary and Cultural Theory*. 3rd ed. Manchester: Manchester University Press, 2009.

Barton, Robert. *Style For Actors: A Handbook for Moving Beyond Realism.* 2nd ed. New York: Routledge, 2009.

Brockett, Oscar G. and Franklin J. Hildy. *History of the Theatre.* 10th ed. Boston, MA: Pearson, 2008.

Castagno, Paul C. *New Playwriting Strategies: A Language Based Approach to Playwriting.* New York: Routledge, 2001.

Crawford, Jerry, Catherine Hurst, and Michael Lugering. *Acting: In Person and in Style.* 5th ed. New York: McGraw-Hill, 1994.

de Heer, Rolf (dir.) "The Bandala and the Bark Canoes." *Ten Canoes.* DVD. Palm Pictures and Film Finance Corporation Australia, 2006.

Fuchs, Elinor. "Waiting for Recognition: An Aristotle for 'Non-Aristotelian' Drama." *Modern Drama,* 50.4 (Winter 2007): 532–44.

Gassner, John and Edward Quinn. *The Reader's Encyclopedia of World Drama.* Mineola, NY: Dover, 2002.

Harrop, John and Sabin R. Epstein. *Acting with Style.* 3rd ed. Boston, MA: Allyn and Bacon, 1999.

Janson, Anthony F. *Janson's History of Art.* 7th ed. Boston, MA: Prentice Hall, 2006.

Miller, Arthur. *Salesman in Beijing.* London: Methuen, 2005.

Mirriam-Webster Online. Dictionary. <www.merriam-webster.com/>. Cited November 16, 2009.

Russell, Douglas A. *Period Style for the Theatre.* 2nd edn. Boston, MA: Allyn and Bacon, 1987.

Thomas, James. *Script Analysis for Actors, Directors, and Designers.* 4th ed. Boston, MA: Focal, 2009.

Trousdell, Richard. "Directing as an Analysis of Situation." *Theatre Topics,* 2 (March 1992): 25–39.

Zarrilli, Phillip B. *Psychophysical Acting: An Intercultural Approach after Stanislavski.* London: Routledge, 2009.

Index